103 FUNDRAISING IDEAS FOR PARENT VOLUNTEERS WITH SCHOOLS AND TEAMS

Cathy McGough

Stratford Living Publishing

WHAT READERS ARE SAYING

From the USA

"I was very impressed with this book and the amount of information it covered. This is a wonderful source of information on planning events and deciding on the right event for the organisation. So next time you are looking to raise money for your school or organisation, don't go with the usual – take a look in Cathy McGough's book and consider new ideas that will excite the community!"

FIVE STARS READERS FAVOURITE

"This should be in every school! An excellent guide for schools and camps."

FIVE STARS AMAZON READER

INSPIRATION

"Unless someone like you cares a whole lot,
nothing is going to get better.
It's not."
Dr. Seuss
"Volunteers are the only human beings on the face
of the earth who reflect this nation's compassion,
unselfish caring, patience,
and just plain loving one another."
Erma Bombeck
"Great things are done by a series of small things brought
together."
Vincent Van Gogh

MORE INSPIRATION

"We make a living by what we get but we make a life
by what we give."
Winston Churchill
"No one is useless in this world
who lightens the burdens of another."
Charles Dickens
"If we did all the things we were capable of,
we would astound ourselves."
Thomas Edison
"It is when you give of yourself that you truly give."
Khalil Gibran
"I alone cannot change the world, but I can cast
a stone across the waters to create many ripples."
Mother Teresa

TABLE OF CONTENTS

INTRODUCTION

This award-winning resource (2016 3rd Place Best Reference Category Metamorph Publishing SIBA Awards) offers creative solutions for schools, clubs, teams, non-profits, and community groups of all shapes and sizes.

In addition to volunteering both as a member of schools and teams Fundraising Organisations, and as a Fundraising Co-ordinator, Cathy McGough is an award-winning fundraiser. She led the combined team of staff and volunteers at Lifeline Sydney and Sutherland, in Australia with two successful campaigns:

1/ 2008 City of Sydney Charity of the Year Business Award

2/ 2008 Non-Government or Community Organization Category Mental Health Association NSW.

Packed with suggestions and updated after the recent covid events, Cathy offers suggestions   based upon real-world inspiration and experience. This book helps organizers at every level – whether you are planning a or replacing an old fundraising event you will not be let down.

FOREWORD

Dear *Parents, Friends & Volunteers,*

The purpose for writing this book, was to help parents who are seeking ways to contribute to their children's education. Parents who are on a variety of committees, whether it be for soccer teams, or hockey teams or pre-schools or private or public schools and with across-the-board cuts in funding - the only way to achieve the tools your children need in order to succeed is to work together as teachers/coaches and parents in committees and to set achievable goals so that you can raise the required money yourselves.

In the past, through using a combination of many of these fundraising ideas we have been able to reach and sometimes even exceed our own expectations. Here is a list of only some of things we have been able to achieve as a group over the years:

*We re-stocked our school library.

*We funded the part time salary so our school could have a music teacher.

*We raised funds for an upgrade in school computers.

*We raised funds for an air conditioning unit.

*We raised funds for additional storage for the school.

*We raised funds for necessary renovations.

*We funded yearly gifts for the graduating class.

*We raised funds for on-site musical instruments to assist the music teacher.

*We raised funds for a teacher and boards for an after-school chess club.

*We raised funds for an after-school language program including a teacher.

*We raised funds for a full school Fitness program.

The list goes on and on, and what you can achieve is only limited to your own imagination.

Read on – 103 Fundraising Ideas await you!

So, go on! What are you waiting for? Go fundraise!

Yours,

Cathy McGough

INSPIRATION

"Never doubt that a small group of thoughtful,
committed citizens can change the world.
Indeed, it is the only thing that ever has."
Margaret Mead.

"Those who bring sunshine to the lives of others
cannot keep it from themselves."
J. M. Barrie

To all the wonderful volunteer parents...
YOU ROCK!
Together we make magic happen every single day.

LET'S GET STARTED

GOALS AND BUDGET

A s a fundraiser it is understood – your goal is to raise funds for your child's school or team.

First you need to know what services and/or upgrades are required.

What is your overall goal?

How are you going to get there...with minimal financial outlay.

How will you manage upfront costs? For example, renting a hall for an event.

"Pay attention to where you are going because without meaning you might get nowhere."
A. A. Milne

LOOKING AHEAD

ESTABLISHING GOALS

The easiest way to determine what is required, is to meet with the Principal, or Coach and make a Wish List of everything the children need.

Be realistic.

Especially if this if the first year a team has been put together to fundraise.

If this isn't the first year, then you'll have a track record of successes (and failures), and this will help you to put together a Fundraising Budget.

FINANCIAL GOALS

FUNDRAISING BUDGET

A s with any other budget, you will need to include listings for all individual costs including projections. Good budgeting and planning will ensure that you keep your spending in gear.

If for example your school needed items adding up to $20,000.00 – you'd plan Events and Social Activities, with projections for each.

This may sound overwhelming – but keep reading for specific ideas you can add to the list and implement into your budget.

LET'S BREAK IT DOWN

OVERVIEW

INDIVIDUAL EVENT BUDGET AND GOALS

As you move through the 103 Fundraising Ideas, take note of which ideas you think would work well in your environment. Choose the ones which make you feel excited, while at the same time they feel practical – that they would work for you and your child's school and/or team. Make a TOP 10 list of these ideas as a starting point. Narrow it down with the help of those around you including Principals, Teachers, Coaches...then filter down their input to your team of volunteers once you have a team in place. There might be a way you can incorporate many of the 103 Fundraising Ideas into a larger event.

BREAK EACH EVENT DOWN

From your TOP 10 LIST, choose each event and break them down.

Create an itemized list of what you'll require with projected expenses. This is an exercise which is imperative to go through, whether you use the idea or not at this time.

There are many FREE sites online to help you make a budget using a spreadsheet will help you keep organized. It's key to update regularly. Remember the more information you have the better.

Once you know where you're going – there are ways in which you can try to get donations for as many items as you can. More on this also coming up.

Your Treasurer (once you have one in place on your team) should set up a policy for all aspects of money handling at events. More on this later. See the separate heading for Money for a breakdown of these areas.

FUNDRAISING RECORDS

Most Parent Volunteer Committees change yearly since leaders are elected for a term.

That shouldn't stop you from setting up long term goals and keeping records which will help the next incoming group of volunteers.

PUBLICITY AND SOCIAL MEDIA

Using Social Media if you're a non-profit organization doesn't cost anything at the moment.

Once your school or team has their social media setup, you can schedule in fundraising event news, etc., with their postings.

You can set up parent/volunteer groups.

Connect with families. Connect with friends.

Ask for help.

Build a community.

This is a key part of your pre- and post-marketing plan.

Your contact at the school or team, will have an image to maintain and they will have either a volunteer or staff member who regularly updates the site, makes regular postings, answers, questions, etc.

It takes time to set up and to maintain and you can be a part of the school's scheduled postings.

It's best if you have one person from your team of volunteers who will regularly be in touch with, update and inform the person who is the Media Coordinator for your child's school or team. Developing a strong relationship with that person, could be key to the success of your event.

Social Media is also an excellent platform to attract volunteers, but your website, newsletter, and bulletin board also present opportunities to attract attention and bring new people on board.

There are probably quite a few Free Event Calendars for your community which you can access on-line and upload the information for your fundraising event.

Don't forget to contact local television stations, newspapers, and radio stations.

Preparing and sending a Press Release is an amazingly effective way of informing the media about your event.

If you're not familiar with writing a Press Release, there are a few options you can take:

#1. Ask your team of volunteers if they have expertise in this field (or if they know someone who might help.)

#2. Ask if any of the parents has expertise in this field. This can be done via a newsletter, a posting on the school or team's website, or at a school event parents attend like the weekly assembly or a game.

#3. Check for templates on-line. Free and paid for templates are available on-line. Do a search and you'll be able the best option to suit your needs.

#4. Hire a professional (perhaps barter their services, or offer them publicity at your event. Or ask if their company might be able to write a Press Release Pro Bono.

DON'T FORGET TO

PERMISSIONS AND PRE-EVENT PLANNING

I can't tell you enough how important it is, for you to check with your local Council, City, State, Province or any other municipal body to ensure that you have all of the correct information, permissions, licenses, etc. before you set the date for your event.

You might have to apply in order to hold a public event in a public place, or for special licenses (food handling, alcohol, etc.), and you might require additional insurance. These are just some of the Permissions you could require, and it is best to know what you are dealing with before you get in too deep with your event.

If you don't follow the rules, then two things could happen:

#1. You get fined.

#2. You have to cancel your event.

If #2 happens, it might make it impossible for you to get approval to hold your event again in the future.

It is particularly important for you to have regular correspondence and a contact with your local Council. Keep excellent records. Ensure that you have dotted all your I's and crossed all of your T's before you set your plan into motion - and then this is something you won't have to worry about again.

There is nothing worse than having promoted your event, sold tickets, attained sponsors and donation, and then having to cancel your event. Stating OOPs after the fact will not gain you or your cause any credibility.

This message will be repeated on and off throughout this book as a reminder. Always keep this message in the back of your mind even if it isn't mentioned.

"If you want to go fast, go alone. If you want to go far, go with others."

African Proverb

I GET BY WITH A LITTLE HELP

TEAM TIME!

YOUR TEAM OF VOLUNTEERS

Whether you have been elected to your role as fundraising coordinator or it has been thrust upon you (because no one else put up their hand) it doesn't really matter. You will need a firm team of volunteers, most who probably did not want to take on the role for themselves. This will hopefully work in your favour - because they will have empathy and be even more supportive.

CHOOSE WISELY

Volunteers are critical to the success of the fundraising event. It's important to make everyone feel welcome and needed and to be able to delegate tasks. It's also important that your volunteers choose to work on an area of the project, which they feel they have the strongest skill, and interest in.

TEAM TIME

Once you have a group of volunteers, you need to check time, availability, and an effective way to do this is through regularly scheduled meetings. Communication is key and everyone will have something unique and individual to offer.

Once the team is in place, you need to work together and create an environment where everyone will want to offer ideas and opt to put in the necessary time.

THE BIG PICTURE
Setting Goals Together
Use mutual goals to motivate your volunteers.

Encourage the more experienced volunteers in your group to pass on their knowledge to new volunteers.

Inspire new volunteers to offer ideas from their perspective; sometimes-new volunteers are the ones who are best able to think outside of the box.

As I mentioned before, most key roles will be elected and for a term such as:

TREASURER
SECRETARY
FUNDRAISING CO-ORDINATOR
BACKUP FUNDRAISING COORDINATOR
GRANT APPLICATION COORDINATORS (2)
VOLUNTEER COORDINATOR & TRAINER
MARKETING   MATERIALS/PUBLICITY
COORDINATOR.

ANSWERABLE TO:
Fundraising will be one of the committee functions, and as a team you will more than likely report to the Committee's President, Vice President, in addition to key members of your child's school or team such as The Principal and/or the Coach.

Keeping those who you are answerable to updated on progress, and goals will be critical to the success of your fundraising team and events.

Regularly scheduled Committee Meetings will allow you, the Fundraising Coordinator, the opportunity to update them, to get them excited about up-and-coming events and most importantly to bring them on board in helping and supporting said event.

You'd also have your Year Budget approved through this avenue.

"We make a living by what we get,
But we make a life by what we give."
Winston Churchill

"There is no "I" in team, but we sure are glad
there is a "U" in volunteers."
Author Unknown

LEADERSHIP

MEETINGS

LEADING MEETINGS

When you setup meetings for your fundraising team, remember that your volunteers are taking time away from their families (like you are) in order to help.

Make sure this time is well planned and stick to an agenda.

Send out or post an agenda prior to the meeting.

Have cookies, cake, water, tea, and coffee at a minimum available for refreshments. On special occasions a bottle of Champagne might even be in order to celebrate a group achievement

Invite everyone to attend and make it a safe environment in which anyone feels free to offer their suggestions and opinions.

Encourage participation but don't forget to take control of the situation - lead - and keep everyone on track.

By sticking to the time limit you've allotted, volunteers will be more inclined to attend future meetings.

If you go way over your allowed schedule each time because people get off-track, then word will get around.

Value the time of your volunteers – and your own.

Have fun, but keep to a schedule and volunteers will be more likely to continue attending meetings.

"Kindness like a boomerang, always returns."
Author Unknown

"Every action in our lives touches on some chord that will vibrate in eternity."
Edwin Hubbell Chapin

ROLE PLAYING

VOLUNTEER TRAINING

TRAINING

Some volunteers might feel uncomfortable about asking businesses for donations.

A role-playing session with volunteers, going through the process is always helpful.

A suggestion you might want to try, is role playing. Make it fun and let everyone have a go at both being the Store Owner and being the volunteer.

Go through the process, step by step, then switch roles. This will be the confidence of all involved and the role reversal will help to see from all perspectives.

You also want to ensure that the person who will be approaching businesses is professional about it. They should look the part, dressed in clean attire. After all they are representing your child's school. They should also have proof that they request is legitimate.

(See sample letter in the Trivia Night Event.)

It's also important for your volunteers to understand if the business says no, they shouldn't take it personally or make the owner feel bad.

Asking businesses for donations gets easier and easier the more you do it.

I always look at this way – if the business is able to donate, then why not to your child's school or team?

INTERESTS
Areas of Expertise and Interest

Make certain you dedicate areas to each of the volunteers and that they know their particular area and boundaries.

Nothing is more embarrassing (and annoying to the store owner) than to have two or three volunteers from the same school and/or team approach their businesses for donations one after the other.

It looks very unprofessional.

If it does happen – ensure your volunteer is ready with an apology and a thank you for the business owners time.

"Volunteers do it for free."
Author Unknown

WHAT'S IN IT FOR ME?

TRIED AND TRUE

WHAT WORKS...

1. Approach the business. Introduce yourself (at a time when the business owner isn't busy with other customers. If they are busy, then come back or wait your turn.) Tell them the name of your school (or team) and give them a signed letter from the Principal or Coach.

2. Explain about your event, date, fundraising goals (which should also be explained in the letter) and ask for a donation for a prize, silent auction, etc.

WHAT'S IN IT FOR THEM

Tell them upfront how it will benefit their business.

For example:

*Their business will be mentioned in the program which will be handed out at the event

*Their business will be announced during the event by the Master of Ceremonies.

*Their business will be listed on Social Media promotions

*Their business logo will be included on posters at the event

*The name of their business, location and phone number will be included on a placemat at each of the tables at the event.

3. Inform the business owner that you will come back later in the week (name the day) to see if they have anything to donate.

This means they don't feel like they have to decide on the spot. Some need to check the budget or stock; some need to check with a partner.

Make sure you make a note of when you said you're return – and that you do go back.

APPROACHING BUSINESSES

4. Collect the donation. Say thank you. Record what was donated.

KEY TIP #1
Tell all the businesses you'll return on the same day. Don't give a specific time.

KEY TIP #2
Ask for a business card and attach it to the item. If you're collecting a lot of donations – you want to ensure the thank you is attributed to the correct business.

If the person you spoke to isn't there or they don't have anything ready, they might ask you to come back on another day.

Choose a day and return for any other donations on that day. Refer to Key Tip #1. Plan all revisits on the same day.

Note: sometimes you have to go back quite a few times to get donations. Remember you're not the only school or team which will be asking for help.

Keep this in mind, and be patient and understanding with the business.

THE UNEXPECTED

If the unexpected happens – where something meant for your school was accidentally given to another – make sure the business owner is left with a good impression of you and your child's school or team by being polite and saying thank you.

If you receive a donation, make sure you follow up after the event with a Thank You Certificate. Tell them how much money you raised. Thank them personally once again.

KEY TIP #3
You can never say thank you too many times.

RESPECT

IT'S MUTUAL

Fundraising for schools and teams is highly competitive.

Ensure the business owner feels good about it, so when someone walks in next year instead of you, he or she will remember.

5. If the business owner says that he/she can't help this year, don't make him/her feel bad.

Business owners can't support every school or team which asks for help. Keep in mind, business owners also have sons and daughters who are attend local schools and play on local teams. Needless to say - they can't support every cause.

Say thank you and that you'll check back in next year if that's okay with them.

Shake their hand and walk away – always leaving a good impression.

"Nobody can do everything,
but everyone can do something."
Author Unknown

VISION

PLAN – PLAN – PLAN!

When you're holding a fundraising event (especially a large one) you will want to put together a schedule for the event and find a person for every job.

Who will setup and decorate the hall beforehand?

Who will greet people at the door?

Who will sell tickets?

Who will manage the Raffles? Auction? Silent Auction?

Go through everything and put in a time and a volunteer (or two) to manage each and everything that you know will be happening. If you need more volunteers – this is the best time to ask for them instead of scrambling at the last moment.

Planning and follow-up will be key to motivating and inspiring your team.

Always remember that they have your back (and make sure that you have theirs.)

"Alone we can do so little -
together we can do so much."
Helen Keller

ASKING FOR HELP

MEET THE PARENTS

VOLUNTEERS

If your school has a Parent & Teacher Meeting (or your team) then this is the best place to look for parents who are interested in getting involved. Generally, people who attend these meeting are looking for ways in which they can use their skills in order to help their children.

Perhaps you've had conversations with other parents, who say there's no way they'd attend the annual meeting – because they don't have time to fill any role.

Most parents don't have time – but someone has to step up. Stepping up is less frightening when you have a good team of volunteers around you.

If you're only interested in Fundraising – not the major committee terms – then if nominated, you can affiliate yourself with the appropriate subcommittee of volunteers.

Primarily, the key committee as discussed would include:

1. Leader (President)

2. Co-leader (Vice President)
3. Treasurer
4. Secretary
5. Fundraising Coordinator

After these positions have been designated, a subcommittee for fundraising can be established with a team of willing volunteers.

MORE LEADERSHIP

SET A ROUTINE

FUNDRAISING MEETINGS

In your first fundraising meeting request that the head of the school, or the coach come prepared with a list of fundraising goals they would like to be achieved during that year. This has been mentioned previously, but how to incorporate it into a specific meeting was not.

After the list is presented, meet with your fundraising group and brainstorm ideas for how to achieve those monies.

In your second meeting, ask the head of the school or coach to attend. Run the ideas your team have come up with and present your projections. If it's not possible to achieve the goals set, change them. Adjust accordingly. Then make a rough plan.

Now that you have a fundraising plan outline in place, you need to map out the when's and the where's. You also need to map out the how's - as in how many more volunteers you are going to need. You then, need to include in either the school or team's newsletter your fundraising plan and to ask for assistance. This is an excellent time to sell your plan, let everyone know how they can help and to start promoting your first event.

It would be appropriate to have no more than one or two larger fundraisers per year.

KEY TIP #4
Don't put all your eggs into one basket.

Those two major events will be the fundraisers from which you will raise the majority of your funds.

Therefore, both events must be successful events.

Those be the most costly timewise and they will require the most financial outlay pre-event.

SELECTING A VENUE

Before you book your venue, make sure you go there in person to ensure the space is suitable.

Take a pen and paper with you – and map out how things might look at your event.

How many tables will fit it? Then you'll know how many tickets you can sell and how many teams you'll need in order to sell out.

Make sure there is space at the entryway for tables, plenty of electrical outlets, suitable lighting, kitchen facilities (if required), space to set up Silent Auction and display prizes.

If you're able to network with another school and rent their auditorium cheaply (or free of charge) then mapping it out in advance will save you time and headaches in the long run.

It's all down to budget. If you can save money on the venue – it'll keep your overhead down.

PLAN AHEAD
Once you choose the venue – BOOK IT.
CONFIRM THE DATE.
LOCK IT IN.

Make sure parents know about these events way in advance so they mark the date in their calendars.

Get the ball rolling – i.e., publicize your event, on all avenues, to ensure no one else in your area chooses the same date as yours.

If both events are successful, pen them in for the next year at the same time.

Even if the event doesn't make as much money as you hoped the first time around, don't admit defeat straight away. Learn from your mistakes and make it better next time. Some events require momentum.

"You just never give up. You do a task to the best of your abilities and beyond."
Debbie Reynolds

EVENTS
SECONDARY EVENTS
Choose other events from the list of 103 Fundraising Events. Each will bring in money – some might even surprise you as to how much.

Keep in mind the valuable time you will be asking from your volunteers and don't ask them to do too much. Remember volunteers have families and commitments too. You don't want them to overdo it.

Make sure your core team, doesn't become elitist. Always state that everyone is welcome. Encourage people to sit in on your meetings and to offer suggestions. Make it easy for people to want to help and to get involved.

HAVE FUN!

True raising funds is the goal – but having FUN is a necessity!

"Act as if what you do makes a difference.
It does."
William James

VOLUNTEER APPRECIATION DAY

BOOK IT-WIN WIN!

Who should plan a Volunteer Appreciation Day?

Some say the school or team should. But what if they don't?

Then it's up to you as the leader.

KEY TIP #5
Always include a Volunteer Appreciation Day Event on your plan.

If your school or team plans an event too – then your volunteers get two celebrations in their honour. Which they deserve. And you as leader will also get a pack on the back. WIN WIN.

WHAT IS A VOLUNTEER APPRECIATION DAY?

This is where the volunteers are able to sit back and relax while they are pampered and thanked.

It is good to offer them a physical thank you in the form of a letter or something more symbolic like a ribbon.

Perhaps the children could make something for them? Or sing them a song?

ON-ON-ONE THANK YOUS!

Ask the principal or coach to personally thank all the volunteers. A handshake or a personal thank you will mean a lot to your volunteers.

KEY TIP #6
As committee lead you should be thanking your volunteers all the time. Every single day.

"If you become a helper of hearts,
springs of wisdom will flow from your heart."
Rumi

"Volunteers are love in motion!"
Author Unknown

GETTING INVOLVED

PARTICIPATION IS KEY!

WHO MIGHT YOUR VOLUNTEERS BE?

There is nothing better for your child, than to have his/her parents involved through volunteering with his school or team.

It's true, children do learn what they see. Perhaps your involvement will one day inspire them to be involved int their own child's school or team.

KEY TIP #7.
Everyone loves to be asked.
And you never know until you do.
So, ask parents to help. In any way they possibly can.

This can also be achieved through non-fundraising events for parents who want to assist teachers or to get involved in before, during or after school programs.

When the children see that you take the time out to volunteer to help their school or team, they are more than likely as adults to volunteer too.

You are always setting an example for your children.

You have unique skills, which only you can bring to the table.

Don't be afraid to ask if there are other ways in which you can help.

STUDENTS
Student Volunteers

If the children on your team or at your school are old enough, they would be excellent additions to your volunteering team.

Ensure that they receive training and understand the task and procedures. It might also be an innovative idea, to set up a mentoring system with an experienced volunteer and a student.

Working together with the same goals will create an even stronger community for all involved.

"We cannot always build the future for our youth,
but we can build our youth for the future."
F. D. Roosevelt

BEFORE THE MEETING

GET ORGANIZED!

PRE-EVENT MEETINGS

O nce you have your team and plan for your fundraising events, you'll want to set up subcommittees.

If you're planning two major events, everyone should be involved in these – i.e., all hands-on deck.

Subcommittees can focus manage on the smaller events, ensuring once a plan is in place. They can also attend meetings to discuss needs and progress.

As Fundraising Coordinator you'll be heading up the plan, and you'll be involved in every single committee. Use your Fundraising Plan as a guideline for your meetings.

Ask leaders of each branch of your volunteering team to offer up a Progress Report on each of the areas which they are responsible for.

Having regular meetings will keep everyone on track and assist you in reaching achieving the school/team's financial goals.

Sent out benchmarks, and work as a team to reach them. Working together will keep everyone motivated and excited about the project.

Don't be afraid to change gears if you find something isn't working.

Keep excellent records, this will be invaluable for future reference.

"We cannot live only for ourselves.
A thousand fibers connect us with our fellow men."
Herman Melville

TEAMS

IS THIS RIGHT FOR ME?

LEADERSHIP

Whether you are President of Fundraising, Committee Lead or just the parent who raised their hand to run a fundraising campaign for a school or team - you will be leading the ship.

You might ask yourself a few questions before taking on the commitment such as:

IS THIS RIGHT FOR ME?

Once you decide to put yourself forward for the lead role, others will rally around you. If elected, you'll step into the spotlight knowing you have won the support of others in the school community.

Now that you are official, the most important thing to remember is that you are not alone.

If you are the take charge kind of person, who likes running the show - then that is all good. Keep in mind the time commitment and don't be afraid to ask for help.

It will eat into your family time and your time with friends, and it will require your full attention at times when you may be needed elsewhere.

When this happens, you need a good, dedicated team behind you, people you can count on and delegate to.

It is well worth repeating:

You are not alone.

"Volunteering is the ultimate exercise in democracy. When you volunteer,
you vote every day about the kind of community you want to live in."

AUTHOR UNKNOWN

MEETINGS

MAKE A PLAN

Once all officials have been elected are in place, together you need to put together a plan.

Your school or team can tell you what is needed in the oncoming year. How many funds are required.

Now, using the ideas in this book, you can put together a plan and a timeline.

Regular meetings will help get things moving. In addition to creating a bond between staff, volunteers, and team.

An agenda is imperative.

Hitches along the way will happen, they must be discussed and sorted immediately.

If your team needs to steer into a different direction, early discovery of impacting issues will be key.

Constantly change and update your plan and timelines, as they are living documents. Make sure everyone is clear on what their job is, when they are expected to complete it by and most importantly, make sure that they have the right training and tools to be able to do whatever it is that they are needed to do.

As discussed previously, you may wish to have a meeting initially with your school or team to discuss the fundraising needs for the up-and-coming year.

Then as team leader, you can brainstorm with your members and decide on what fundraising events you are going to tackle in order to reach the goals and ensure the children have everything they need.

Monthly meetings will work at first, but as you get closer to your event, you may wish to change to weekly meetings. As the day approaches, daily meetings may be required.

It is important to keep everyone's spirits up and to tackle any concerns as they happen. You've got this!

KEY TIP #8
Thank goodness for email and internet meeting places, both in groups and live you can easily manage all your meetings – even daily.
When time is ticking on, you'll appreciate these wonderful connecting social media outlets even more.

KUDOS!

THANK YOU!

From the very first time you meet and an impression on your potential fundraising volunteers - make it clear you are running a ship where everyone's ideas are heard and appreciated.

Encourage everyone to step into the spotlight.

Don't be afraid to delegate.

Or to ask for help when needed.

Minutes of all meetings are important.

Always ensure someone is keeping a record and make sure all attendees receive a copy promptly after the meeting ends. Send a copy to the person who represents the school and team at your committee meeting to ensure they are kept in the loop.

This will be key to keeping all of your fundraising events (and volunteers) on track.

BE APPRECIATIVE! THANK YOUR TEAM

(Yes, I already said it – but it's worth repeating!)

Don't forget to praise and thank your team for all the time they are spending to reach the school or team's goals.

At the close of the event, always call your team up onto the stage.

Introduce them one by one, praising them for their contribution.

Ask them to take a bow too. You can be side by side for the well-earned standing ovation.

"How wonderful it is that nobody need wait a single moment before starting to improve the world."
Anne Frank

THE BIG PICTURE

GRANTS, PROPOSALS, ETC.

There may be other fundraising streams available within your community through your local or regional council, foundations, trusts, and corporations.

To be in a position to apply for these you must be tapped into your community.

Specialized Team

To ensure that your school or team doesn't miss out on potential funding, you may wish to add a specialized team of volunteers to work on this specific project.

Reading and following the guidelines for grants requires someone who has time and keen attention to detail.

By allocating this role to one or two volunteers you'll have a better chance to ensure that your school/team meets all the necessary requirements and adheres to the grant rules for each of the organizations.

Your team should report at regular Pre-Event Meetings and update everyone.

This should also be the time to request help if they should require assistance from principals/coaches and/or additional volunteers in order to fulfill their duties.

APPLICATION RULES
GUIDELINES &
CRITERIA

First, make sure that your team checks to ensure that your school or team is eligible to apply for the grant. If your team is uncertain, encourage them to call. By asking in advance they will not only save themselves a whole lot of time and trouble, but it will also show that they respect the time and purpose of the organization which you potentially may partner with. In some cases, you might not qualify for the grant you were planning to go for; instead, they may redirect your efforts towards something more suitable.

Many of these applications will require you to apply every single year. Some years you may be successful, others you may not. However, you should always put in an application and hope for the best.

Some organizations (if you are lucky) might even get in touch with your organization and invite you to send in an application. This means that the word is out about the work you do. Relationships with any/all of these organizations can be invaluable. Network with them, get to know them and let them get to know your organization and what you do for the community.

Check to ensure you have the latest application.

Fill in the application in its entirety and make sure you have it in before the deadline. Last minute is never good when you're filling in what might be a complex application for funds in an extremely competitive environment.

Make your school/team stand out. Tell what is unique about you and why. Give a brief overview about how your school/team started and whom you help and how you help them in the community. Make them want to invest in your school or team.

Ensure you follow their rules and give them all of the information they have requested. Not filling in an answer would mean a no to your application. Respect the process - make sure you have answered every question.

Tell them what you need the money for. What the money will be used for. Tell them why the funding is required and how it will better things for the children at your school or on your team.

Have a plan for your project with firm information in place. In this highly competitive venture having a vision will be the key to your success.

When you are requesting money for a certain project, you need to have a sum in mind. Including an itemized list of the things you will need will show commitment on your part. A budget, including the money your group intends to invest and/or other monies and how you are going to get them and how you researched and forecasted your budget.

Make sure the principal and/or coach sees and approves the application before it is sent off to the organization. Include a letter with the application thanking the organization for the opportunity to tell them about your school/team.

If you get the funding - awesome. Make sure you follow through with all the mandatory requirements and that you thank the organization for choosing to assist your school/team.

Invite a representative from this organization to your Annual Volunteer Appreciation Day so they can meet and mingle with all of your amazing volunteers.

Publicly thank the organization in every way possible.

Present them with a Certificate of Appreciation for their help.

Make them feel like they a part of your team (because they are!)

Doing these things can make your organization stand out and will hopefully help build a strong partnership which will last over time.

SCHOOL OR TEAM WEBSITE

Fundraising should be included as a part of your school or team website menu. It is not advisable to set up something separately as it could be very expensive and also difficult to maintain. Since you are fundraising for the needs and requirements of your school it would definitely be counterproductive.

You can, however, create your own website on many platforms for free. However, maintenance and updates would require a big commitment from your volunteers. In addition to the time commitment, you may also have to train volunteers to set it up, update it, etc.

Using Social Media might be the best platform for you. Check out the chapter on Publicity and Social Media for additional information.

MONEY

Before you start fundraising for your school or team, you should be fully knowledgeable about the school (or team) and provincial as well as federal rules in regard to how the funds should be managed and where they should be deposited. This is as much for your protection as for the protection of those whom you are fundraising for. If the school or team does not have set policies in place, then this should be brought to the attention of The Principal and/or Coach, and a system should be put in place prior to the start of fundraising.

The school should have in place:

Cash Handling Procedures

Accounting Procedures

Deposit of Funds Procedures

Treasurer Procedures

Bank Account for the Purpose of Fundraising Procedures (setting up an established account if one has not already been opened for the specific purposes of fundraising deposits)

- Bank Account Signing Procedures

- Routine Auditing Procedures

- Reporting of Funds Procedures

- Cash Flow/Floater Procedures

- Cheques/Copies of Cheques Cashing and Tracking Procedures

- Giving Receipts On, and After Events

- Procedures for Fundraising Profit Storage After

Event (Locked Deposit Box)

• Insurance/Coverage for Fundraising Protection

In addition to the list above, your country or province/state might have specific laws in regard to the maximum amount you can spend on fundraising expenses. The list included, advises on how to keep your overhead low, but if you know what the law is, and can work within it from the beginning then your efforts will be realistic and profits in line with the actual amounts you are able to raise.

Example: if in Year 1 you do not know about the maximum ceiling and spend 50% in your event on expenses.

You have a successful event and are happy with profit, but when you can only spend for example 15% by law on fundraising expenses then it will be difficult to tighten your belt and hold a similar event with such a decrease in budget.

Especially after the first fundraising event your guests will have elevated expectations.

It is critical to know the laws and policies in advance and meet all their requirements.

Also critical is finding out about taxation including receipts before you begin fundraising.

ALCOHOL

For some of the events on this list, serving alcohol is suggested. It is up to you, the fundraiser to ensure this suggestion is a good "fit" for your team or school. It is also up to you to ensure that you meet all of the local, provincial/state, and federal laws.

In all cases, if alcohol is involved, please ensure that there is a Don't Drink and Drive campaign and a Designated Driver campaign. Also, it would be a good idea to have a local taxi company available after your event should their services be required.

No event wants to end in tragedy. Planning your event includes keeping your guests entirely safe and getting them to and from your event safely.

PREMISES

When you are choosing a location for your event, depending on what the event is you may have specific requirements that need to be met. For example:

- Wheelchair Accessible

- Child Care

- Transportation

- Dietary Requirements

- Multi-language/Translation

To name but a few. You know your school/team, so if you have anything to add to this list specific to you, please address it and find out how you can solve it before you close a deal on premises. It can make all the difference.

SPONSORSHIPS

Having various levels for sponsorships can really be helpful if you are running a large event. You basically set the sponsors up on tiers. Here is an example of how it could work:

GOLD SPONSOR

This is your top sponsor who will make the highest dollar amount in donations, but they may also donate or assist you with a variety of other necessary skills like promotion, physical donations, etc. Companies on this level, may also have a program in place for their employees to donate their time to your school/team or events as volunteers.

In return, your Gold Sponsor would be promoted on all your event publicities. You would for example include their logo on tickets, your website, social media and you would also promote them on the night of your event. Work out a plan with your Gold Sponsor so that it is a WIN WIN situation for both of you.

Establish a long-term relationship with them and they will stay with you for the course. Don't forget to invite a table of them (5 couples) to your event, have a photographer take their picture. Tweet the photo and put it up on other social media.

Promote their business throughout the evening.

Follow up with a personal thank you in person or on the phone in addition to in writing from The Principal/Coach and a Thank You Certificate.

SILVER SPONSOR

This is your second highest sponsor, and you should promote them on your website and on the night of your event. Offer tickets for 2 couples to attend your event and have a photographer take a picture for the website and include promotion of them during the event perhaps tied in with a specific game or add-event. As above, a personal than you in person or on the phone in addition to in writing from The Principal/Coach and a Thank You Certificate should occur shortly after the event.

BRONZE SPONSOR

Your third highest sponsor: promote on your website. The M.C. could mention their name and thank them with the other sponsors and donors. They should receive a thank you from the Principal/Coach in writing and a Thank You Certificate.

ALL OTHER SPONSORS

If you have an event flyer or placemat scheduled for the night, include the names and logos of the Gold, Silver and Bronze sponsors in size respective to the amounts donated. This is also a good place to highlight the other sponsors who have helped you.

Many people take home these schedules for keepsakes. Make sure it is professionally done and your sponsors will be very happy to be a part of it.

SELFIES AND PHOTOS

While you have guests at your events, you have lots of opportunities to increase the profile of your school or team.

Ask your guests to take selfies and/or group/table shots. Encourage them get involved and to show everyone else how much fun they are having.

Do make sure they ask for permissions before they post of photo of someone else.

If your school or team have their own social media accounts, remind your guests to # hashtag your page too. This way you might even raise funds or get potential new interest in your school or team.

CHEATERS

If you're having a quiz night, there will always be one or two guests who will try to look up the answers.

Remind your guests that this is cheating and if you're caught, you will be fined and say what the amount will be. The fine will be a donation to your fundraiser.

Since everyone is at the event for the same reason – to raise funds for your school or team – telling offenders they'll be fined for the cause upfront is the best policy.

Make sure your MC is aware. Ask everyone to be on the look-out for cheaters. Some might even cheat on purpose and get caught – just to donate more money!

TEMPLATES OR DIY

It's amazing what templates you can find online – and for free including Canva which is highly recommended.

Do a search for:

CORPORATE SPONSORSHIP

THANK YOU TO BUSINESSES

REQUEST FOR CORPORATE DONATIONS.

I've included a sample letter for requesting donations under the Trivia Night Fundraising Idea.

Using a template can be handy, but if you can't find one brainstorming with your team will get the job done.

TIMING IS EVERYTHING

They say that when you are planning an event, timing is everything - and indeed it is.

Whatever event is successful and raises the most funds, other schools or teams will want to take advantage of too. That means, if your event is the last in the line of several others then you will have difficulties ahead (or potential difficulties) with:

SPONSORS AND PRIZES

We all think that our team or school is the only one, but when your volunteers start asking businesses for donations if your event is the last and 4 or 5 (or more) volunteers have been in before you asking for donations - then there is a good chance that the business will be tapped out.

Most local businesses like to support local schools and teams, but sometimes they do exceed their resources, and sometimes other schools and teams will encroach on your territory and get in there first. There's no law against it, so you have to be prepared.

Check out what fundraising events are already scheduled in your area before you choose the date for yours.

Check online for the year previous too.

Try to make your event unique and FIRST.

AFTER EVENT MEETING

After your event, you should always plan to have a meeting of our team. Don't wait too long, or you might forget critical information which will help you with next year's event and/or be deciding factors on whether it would be worthwhile to do the same event again. Schedule your Post Event Meeting no more than 7 days after your event.

SURVEY FOR TEAM MEMBERS

It might be worthwhile to send out a quick survey to all team members who attended asking them to rate your event on a 1-10 scale and for feedback. This information can be useful at your meeting.

DRUM ROLL

THIS IS IT!

A re you ready for the 103 Fundraising Ideas?
    As you read through, stretch your imagination.
  Be prepared to MIX & MATCH to suit your circumstances.
  We're living in a strange time - with this pandemic - but funds are still required.
  I've added suggestions as appropriate to assist you.
  Now get ready to FUNDRAISE!

103 FUNDRAISING IDEAS

1.

TRIVIA NIGHT

Let's start with this idea, because in some ways it is the most complicated event, or it can be if you don't have a plan.

And this event alone can be your bread-and-butter annual event.

It's also an opportunity for me to include the ideas which our team has tried – more than once – and which have worked successfully.

In brackets, I will include the number of the Fundraising Idea which is explained in more details further along in the 103 ideas – so you can see how easy it is to Mix and Match Fundraising Ideas in order to accomplish your goals.

So this is the plan, laid out for your step by step. The How To for your Fundraising Event from start to finish.

Once you have a foundation - the sky is the limit!

The People

First, I would recommend you have a committee of a minimum of 5 people + yourself.

First Things First

Choose a date and time for your event.

Once you have a date and time, you need a location. Hopefully, the school or the sporting event will be able to accommodate you, but if not, you may need to check out local halls, clubs, and schools. You might think the latter is a strange idea, approaching another school for your event, but it is actually a great idea.

Why? If you are a Pre-school and your children will be attending another school soon, it's an excellent way for you to meet other parents and they will be interested in attending your event. It's an excellent way to network. Always look for networking opportunities. Try to get the hall for free. Make sure you ask them about the availability of tables and chairs, kitchen facilities (if needed) and washrooms.

THE PLAN

How do you intend to raise funds?
  1/Sell tickets to The Trivia Night Event - Theme or no?
  2/ Silent Auction
  3/ Raffles
  4/ Games
  5/ Trivia
  6/ Food and Drink

For most of the list above you are going to need donations. This is guaranteed to make your event overhead low.

Here's How:

Now you have the date, and you have the facility you need to start working on prizes. You would be surprised how many businesses are keen to donate prizes; all you have to do is ask them. I would suggest you put one person from your group onto this project.

They should formulate a letter and send it by email to potential donors. At this stage, no business should be crossed off the list. Make an Excel Spreadsheet with the names, contact names, phone number and email address of each of the businesses.

If you do this, the list will be gold for the future.

Sample letter:

Dear Sir/Madam,

XXXXXX School, established in XXXX, is a non-profit organization providing high quality XXXXX at an affordable price to families in the region.

The school is attended by over XX families residing in the following suburbs: LIST SUBURBS.

Fundraising is an essential responsibility for our Committee.

Fundraising enables us to LIST WHAT YOUR GOALS ARE.

Members of our Fundraising Committee are seeking donations in support of
LIST YOUR EVENT NAME AND DATE.

It is the Committee's policy to acknowledge all donors via EXPLAIN HOW YOU WILL ACKNOWLEDGE THEIR DONATION examples - auction newsletter, placement at the event, social media. In addition to this you will receive a "Certificate of Appreciation" from the school.

We would welcome your organization's support of our school as one of its sponsors for YEAR.

Yours sincerely,
YOUR NAME GOES HERE
YOUR SCHOOL/CLUB DETAILS GO HERE

List of Corporate/Institutional Donors

To create a list of potential donors, search for potential donors as an 'A list' of businesses that would benefit from participating.

For example: museums, movie theatres, zoos, and shopping malls. All these businesses will be contacted via email.

Parents can also make donations if they own their own business or work for someone who does.

Don't forget to ask for donations from parents in the newsletter or monthly update from the school or event you are working for.

WALK ABOUT

Divide segments around your event into suburbs or streets and arm your team with the letter above. They should visit each of the local businesses in their area, explaining about your school/or team and the event.

Ask the businesses if they would donate a prize or gift voucher. Some will decide straightaway; others will require a few days to decide. Best plan is to tell them you will drop round on a specific day.

Be friendly and positive, even if they don't donate. Don't make them feel bad or guilty.

Always thank them for their time.

Is Asking for a Donation Begging?

I have been asked this question many times and the answer is always NO.

You are not the only parent asking for a donation from this business.

If they don't say yes to you, then they will say yes to someone else.

So why not you and your event?

Remember the role playing? If not, scroll back. It wouldn't hurt to refresh yourself on the details listed earlier about taking donations.

Plus, in the letter above, you have offered them a benefit, in that their business will be promoted at your event and they will get a Certificate, which they can display in their store.

Most businesses are happy to help. If you are professional and offer them a benefit, then you aren't begging. It is a WIN WIN situation.

Note to Committee Lead –
Anyone who feels this is "begging" after the information above is explained to them should not be visiting businesses face-to-face to ask for donations.

WHAT ELSE TO DO

Create posters to promote your event.
Check out local newspapers to see if they have a free event column.
Call the local radio station see if they will promote your event for free.
Ask the school or event to promote on in their newsletter and put up posters.
Ask parents to help promote the event via their networking partners.
Start selling tickets to your event.

MASTER OF CEREMONIES

Is there a parent who has experience and would be a good Master of Ceremonies for your event? If yes, ask them if they are available.
If no one is suitable, you might need the assistance of a local "celebrity" to take on this role. Perhaps someone from the local radio station might donate his or her time?
If you can't find anyone suitable, the Principal or Coach might love the opportunity to get involved in the fundraiser and be front and centre.
If none of the above work, then please see the next listing Trivia Questions for an alternative suggestion.

TRIVIA QUESTIONS

There are companies who will sell you Trivia Questions and Answers pre-made. You can even choose a specific theme in some cases. Cost varies, but this could save you a lot of time.

Some companies even include a Master of Ceremonies with the package.

Check into this and see if it would suit your event. Would it be worth investing the $ in order to save time over all? Is there room in your budget?

These questions only your committee can answer.

For confidentiality reasons, having the questions and answers managed by an outside company can have definite advantages.

SELLING TICKETS

Once you decide on a price, it is best to ask people to put together a team.

First, look at the hall and decide how many tables will fit and be manageable. Ten is a respectable number, but my recommendation is that tables should have no more than a team of twelve on them.

Remember, you will need to organize a prize for each of the players on the top three teams.

More about this later.

Tickets can be sold in advance or on the night.

When you get a booking for a table, ask the person to choose a name for their team. This can be done on the night, but it will be easier to keep everything organized if you sell tickets and fill tables in blocks of teams.

FOOD AND WINE

Selling food and wine can really complicate your night. If you are selling alcohol you will probably have to apply for a license.

Check with your local government or municipality about this before you promote that alcohol will be available.

One option might be BYO (bring your own) alcohol if the facility is on board with this. You can sell plastic wine glasses. It's good to offer a selection of water and soft drinks.

With food, it is best to keep it simple. A cheese and fruit plate could be made up and added to each table.

SPEAKING OF WHICH...

Make a list of all the supplies you need for the night. There are staple things you'll always need. You can add to the list as and when/needed. Always be prepared to have too much rather than too little on hand:

- Wine glasses

- Napkins

- Cheese

- Crackers

- Pretzels

- Fruit

- Nuts

- Toilet paper

- Paper towels

- Garbage Bags

- Soft Drinks

- Bowls

- Plates

- Straws

- Cups

- Pencils

- Paper

- Raffle tickets

- Receipt book

- Bottle of Scotch

- 12 bottles of wine

- 12 prizes

- 12 wooden spoons

- Jellybeans

- Chocolate Coated Coffee Beans

These are some of the staple things which you'll always need.

If you can get them donated in bulk, you will save time (and money.)

You'll need storage – ask the school to allocate an area and/or ask parents to store items.

For donations check with your local grocery store. If they are a chain, you made need to speak with (and give a letter to) the local Manager who will then pass it on down the line to whoever will make the decision as to which school/team to donate to. Most have monthly budgets (locally) but if your need exceeds what they have on hand (as they already donated to other schools/teams) then time may be required for them to acquire funds from the head office to help you.

GET IN THERE FIRST

The key is to get in to see local businesses first with a letter. Some businesses have a monthly budget to donate to local schools and teams. Some may have to apply for money from their head office.

Some business owners will offer you a gift voucher, which you can use in their store to buy most of the goods listed above.

After you've used every option available for donations, ask parents to donate anything you don't already have. The school or team newsletter is the perfect place to list items and ask for help.

KEY TIP #10
Every time you do your shopping or visit a local business, keep in mind the items on your wish list. Let the person on your team who is allocated to that area know about the business so they can ask for the desired item and follow up if necessary.

DONATIONS COMING IN

Keep an active list of items needed and cross them off as they come in. This should be a different list – of top items required. Items which you will have to purchase yourself if you don't get them donated.

You will receive a lot of donations of items you can use for prizes. Those you will need somewhere to store until the event.

As Fundraising Coordinator, you will need to ensure that you, or someone you delegate to will need to keep track of all donations.

HOW WILL YOU ALLOCATE DONATIONS?

You'll need to decide how to use the selection of donations to raise the most funds such as:

SILENT AUCTION
DOOR PRIZES
RAFFLES
TABLE & GAME PRIZES.

You'll also need to keep a list of which donation was donated by which business for promotion prior and during the event. Also, for thank you purposes after the event.

MICROPHONE

Check with your school to see if they have a microphone for your Master of Ceremonies. If not, check with a nearby school or see if you can rent one or if they'd be happy to donate it to you. Perhaps you have something you can help them with for one of their events?

JUDGES

Three Judges are recommended to make decisions throughout your Trivia Night. They will know the rules and be able to overrule in case of a tie, or settle any disputes in addition to tabulating answers at the end of each round of questions, and confirming winners at the end of the night.

KEY TIP #11

Two judges are plenty, but having three – one as a backup is the smart way to go. You don't want to be trying to find a judge on the night of the event as someone is sick.

GAMES

At the top we alluded to some games. Between rounds when the Judges are tabulating the results it is an excellent time to have some fun and raise some extra money with games.

Here are a few which we found to be successful:
Head and Tails #37
Check Under Your Chair
Count the Jellybeans #15
Liquor Locker #10
Pop a Balloon #14.

SILENT AUCTION (#11)

This will be a big money earner for you, but it takes a lot of organization. You will need to choose the items from donated items and make a bidding sheet. Attendees will bid in increments chosen by you and listed on the bidding sheet in between rounds for items.

The items should be displayed on the same table with the bidding sheets. Bidding sheets should include the item, value, and number of item and leave space for the person bidding to print their name, child's name and class, and bid. If not just for in house bidders, you should also add phone number to the form.

Valuable items, which could be carried off like gift certificates, should not be displayed. Instead, an envelope stating what the gift certificate is for or a photocopy should be on display. This is to avoid items going missing whether through theft or loss.

Your MC should remind people to check their bids between each round. Before the final round, the MC should ask for one last round of bids. When the final round of Trivia is ready to be played, have someone on your team collect the bid sheets.

The winning bids can be tabulated and announced by your MC. At the end of the evening people can claim their prizes, pay what their winning bid amount was, and collect their prize on the way out.

Also make a list of all items up for grabs in the Silent Auction and put that list on each of the tables before the event begins. It's free advertising and will draw attendees to further investigate the items they are interested in and to decide how high they are willing to go to win the item.

CRAPPY GIFTS #13

This is where you ask the parents at the school to donate a "crappy gift" they have received.

This idea was a lot of fun – and an excellent way for parents/teachers to get rid of clutter.

Note: you might want to mention in fun that parents attending the event shouldn't be offended if something they gave is available on the Crappy Gift Table. It happens, so best to mention it upfront.

After all it's a way they can get rid of duplicates, or unwanted new or nearly latest items - all for a worthy cause.

SCRATCHIE TREE #38

In your school or team's newsletter, ask each parent to donate one or more lottery tickets (scratchies) for the purpose of a Scratchie Tree.

What exactly is a Scratchie Tree?

This you can decide for yourself. Suggestions:

If your event is on your near Christmas, you could either draw or use a fake (or real Christmas Tree) and either tape or string up all the lottery tickets. In advance you'd know how many tickets you have. Add up the value of all the tickets combined.

Make this a Silent Auction item which goes to the highest bidder. The Winner takes the tree and all the lottery tickets home.

KEY TIP #12
A photo of the Scratchie Tree can be placed on display at the Silent Auction Table. On the bid form, mention total value paid for Scratchies paid, with the amount possible to win as UNLIMITED or THE SKY'S THE LIMIT.
Keep the actual tree at an agreed location on the premises.
This will save lottery tickets from falling off and/or getting lost during the Silent Auction event.

Head and Tails #37

Place a bowl on each of the tables. We have found plastic bowls work best – especially if alcohol is being served. Less breakage.

Ask all participants to throw a $1.00 coin into the bowl.

You'll need volunteers to collect the money from the bowls for each round.

The Master of Ceremonies will ask questions and participants have to choose whether the answer is a Head or Tails answer.

Participants will be eliminated each round.

The overall winner will receive a prize. The winner will be the last person standing.

Pop a Balloon #14

If you have a lot of small prizes, an effective way to have fun with them by setting up a Pop A Balloon table. Numbers are placed within all balloons. You must write down which number is in each balloon, then allocate a prize for that number.

Customers pay allotted price, choose a balloon, pop it – and they receive the prize designated for that number.

Everybody wins!

Roll a Coin/Coin Toss! #28

Place a bottle of alcohol (Scotch works best) on the floor. Ask attendees to roll a coin (taking turns) toward the bottle. Whoever rolls their coin closest to the bottle wins the bottle.

You could set up two events, one with coin roll and one with coin toss. They both are the same concepts – and a different prize would be allocated.

Have a tape measure on hand, in case two rolls or more seem closest.

Raffles #101

To set up a raffle, you need to sell tickets. This works well if you have larger and more valuable prizes.

Prior to your event, package up prizes and allocate a table on the night to display and promote the raffle.

You'll need a jar or bowl for ticket stubs.

Ask the MC to make an announcement in between rounds so they know volunteers will be selling tickets.

Announce winning tickets via your MC before the final Trivia Round and ask winners to collect their prizes.

CHECK UNDER YOUR CHAIR

After you've set up tables, place a prize under one chair on each of the team's tables.

Ask the MC to tell everyone to look under their chairs. Whoever is sitting in that seat wins the prize.

This is an excellent way to use donations you have left over.

Note: It's not advisable to use this game on every Trivia Night otherwise people will look under their chairs before choosing their seats. Mix it up so they never know when.

Count The Jelly beans (With a Twist) #15

Everyone loves to guess how many jellybeans are in a jar – especially since the winner gets the jar to take home with them.

Here's something different to try – allocate two jars, one with jellybeans for those who are young at heart, and one for the others who prefer something more exotic like chocolate covered coffee beans.

If you have both options available (or one) you'll have to allocate funds to buy the items (and jars.)

Note: you might also get donations from a business for these items if you ask.

Put someone in charge of counting the items in the jar. It's handy to tape the answer under the lid – make sure it's closed tightly. You might even want to put some masking tape around it.

Why?

Because we had one occasion where an attendee decided to open the jar of chocolate covered coffee beans to taste them as they hadn't tried them before. Note: she didn't like them.

To avoid a recount put a masking tape around the jar and keep a close eye on it.

THANK YOU PLACEMATS

KEY TIP #13
When a business donates anything – ask your volunteer to collect a business card. Use the cards, to create placemats – one per person – on every table during the event.

If you're keen on creating Xcel Spreadsheets, then you'll find it easy to create a placemat to promote all of the businesses who've helped by donating a prize.

Type the name, address, and phone number of every business onto the Placemat template. If you want to go fancy, you can have a row of the top donors and include their logo.

At the top of your template include words like:

HELP US TO THANK OUR GENEROUS
Donors and Sponsors
KEY TIP #14
Ask someone – other than the person who created the placemat, to proofread everything before you print out the final copies.

When you visit the businesses, who donated with a Thank You letter and/or Certificate, also bring a copy of the Placement so they can see they were promoted at the event as promised.

It's an excellent way to bring business to those who helped you.

With any lucky they'll come aboard again for next year's event.

TRIVIA PRIZES

You will need prizes for the winning table.

One for each person on the winning team.

*Bottles of Wine are always popular.

(Ask a local restaurant, pub, or winery for donations.)

Second Prize?

If you decide to give out prizes to the team which came in second, you'll need one for each person on that team.

*The same item from the dollar store were always popular at our events.

Worst Table

You would need one prize for each of the team members on the losing team.

*Wooden spoons with ribbons tied around them were always popular items at our events.

ON THE NIGHT

So, the tables are sold out, and everything is setup and ready to go for the night.

You have two people on the door collecting entrance money.

The tables are set up with placements, food, silent auction items, a bowl of coins.

The MC is ready to roll, as are the judges.

You have two people ready to collect money and hand out the Silent Auction items before the night is out.

Now all you have to do is HAVE FUN and watch the money roll in.

Ah, if it was only that easy!

Keep your eyes peeled. Expect the unexpected.

ABOUT THE MONEY

Make sure it is kept safe for each mini event.

Make one of your team responsible for collecting the money after each game.

At the end of the night collect all the money and keep it in a safe.

Put it into the bank as soon as the bank opens.

Let everyone know how much you have earned minus expenses.

What was your goal? Did you reach it?

MEETING

Have a meeting with your team and record what went well and what went wrong and what went well. Make notes of this for next year's committee.

FOLLOW UP

Remember you need to make Certificates of Appreciation for each of the businesses which donated.

For the out-of-town companies or head offices, which gave you donations, you will need to send their Certificate via mail or if they don't mind you can send it via email, and they can print it out themselves.

For local businesses, ideally the same person who collected the donation should visit the business in person.

Don't forget to tell them how much you raised and say THANK YOU in person for their donation.

FUNDRAISING IDEAS

2.

SAUSAGE SIZZLE/HOTDOG SIZZLE

If your children play sports, or you are raising money for a sporting event, then this is the perfect opportunity to raise money.

You can put up a Barbecue near their Saturday games and sell sausages and/or hotdogs.

First check if you require a license from the park. Also check on local places like Malls and Stores who offer organizations the opportunity to raise funds in front of their stores with an event such as this.

What you will need:

Sausages/Hot Dogs
  Buns
  Condiments (Ketchup, Mustard, Relish, BBQ Sauce)
  Onions
  Shredded Cheese

Pickles
Napkins
Soft Drinks
Ice
BBQ
BBQ Implements
Aprons
Water (for washing hands)
Antibacterial soap
Paper Towels
Box of plastic gloves

FOOD DONATIONS:

Approach a local butcher and/or grocery store and request donations any/all of the above items. Get superior quality meat items. Whatever you cannot get donated by the stores, ask parents to donate or buy. Make sure you have a budget in place.

Floater
Put a money floater into place for change. Record how much the floater is and deduct from the profits later.

BBQ and Implements
If you have to bring your own BBQ, arrange for transport to and from the event.

Serving License
Check to see if you need to have a food service license.

When Serving Food

Follow set out food guidelines.

At a minimum:

place the bun a napkin in the palm of your hand.

Put the sausage/hotdog into the bun.

Pass it to the customer.

Allow the customers to add their own condiments.

If there are several customers all at the same time, it might be worthwhile to allocate a volunteer to apply condiments to keep the area clear and the line moving.

FUNDRAISING IDEAS

3.

COSTUME PARTY

This can be tied in with a Trivia Event or can be a separate event.

Ask people to dress up and come to a rented hall or a home if you want to keep it smaller.

You can give prizes for the best and worst costumes.

You can fundraise by playing games.

Check out the section of games and decide which ones you would like to include with your costume party.

You might also wish to include a Movie Night with this one.

FUNDRAISING IDEAS

4.

DANCE

I would suggest you choose a specific era - say eighties music - as a theme and invite people to come wearing clothes from that period of time.

You would need to organize a hall, tables, chairs.

For music, you could hire a D.J. or just put together some play lists on your phone if you have a sound system. It's all down to budget.

To include alcohol, you might need to apply for a license.

Check back to notes for Trivia Night and you can use ideas for games and fun on the night.

FUNDRAISING IDEAS

5.

DIP AND SIP!

I nvite a group of friends over for a session of pampering. As a group, you could decide to do each other's nails, pedicure, hair, etc., to raise money for your school or team. You could include a luncheon, or finger foods if desired.

Alternatively, you could hire these functions out requesting a donation from the profits to your school or team. This would allow everyone to participate.

The Dipping part could be as simple as dipping your feet into a water basin filled with oils.

For the sipping part Champagne is highly recommended.

If you have your Dip and Sip at one of your homes, you will need to have extra towels on hand, but your overhead can remain relatively low.

Things You Need:

- Scented lotions

- Oils

- Rose petals

- Marbles

- Water basins or extra-large bowls

- Seating

- Towels

- Champagne

- Champagne Glasses.

Each attendee will require a bowl or basin large enough to dip their feet into. These can be purchased at the dollar store in bulk.

Having your event outside on a sunny day in the garden would be a lovely environment. Prepare a table with Champagne cooling in a bucket, and glasses at the ready.

Before your guests arrive, set up chairs, with the table nearby. Place a basin in front of each chair and a towel on each seat.

Toss a handful of marbles into each basin so that when guests put their feet in, the marbles will massage the soles of their feet.

When the guests arrive, add warm water, scented oil, and rose petals into each basin.

Open the champagne, pass around the glasses.

Let the pampering begin!

FUNDRAISING IDEAS

6.

CONCERT

You might be thinking hiring a big rock band like U2 might be in order, but that's not what I mean at all.

Local bands need an audience and exposure and often will donate their talent for a fundraiser, which is a cause they relate to. Even better if one of the parents in the band has a child at your school or on your team.

If you have to hire a band, this could make your overhead quite high so I wouldn't recommend this option.

If however you are connected, all you need to do is hire a venue, sell tickets, publicize the concert and let the funds roll in.

Make sure you check if any licenses are required for noise, rubbish collection, etc., from your particular City, Township or Municipality.

FUNDRAISING IDEAS

7.

KARAOKE PARTY

T his is an excellent option if you have someone in your group who has a Karaoke Machine. Otherwise, you can use an online App. coupled with a phone and monitor, then add a microphone and speakers.

A parent from the school might have the expertise you require, otherwise check with local businesses for help.

A local dj might be able to offer his/her services for promotion prior to and on the event night. It's another WIN WIN situation.

Once you have the sound system sorted, choose your date. Lock it in.

You can ask guests to come dressed up as bands or musicians and offer prizes - see above costume party details.

You can incorporate any number of activities including a Silent Auction, Games, etc.

Up to you how big you want this fundraiser to be.

FUNDRAISING IDEAS

8.

BINGO!

Bingo is a fun game for the entire family, but to pull it off you need a Bingo Machine. These can be rented but you might also be able to improvise a machine with a little bit of imagination.

You would then need to purchase books of Bingo Cards and Blotters.

You could request donations and prizes, similar to the Trivia Night and even get someone to MC the night for you.

FUNDRAISING IDEAS

9.

BAKE SALE!

To make this an amazing fundraiser, you need to get outside of your event district and to somewhere customers will be. I suggest you speak to your local shopping center or large chain stores and ask if you could run a Bake Sale out front of their doors on a Saturday morning - their busiest day of the week.

You might need to get a license or food handling permit, check this with your local council.

After you have chosen your day and booked your event location, the next particularly crucial step is to contact a Cake Box (paper company) and ask if they will donate boxes.

For a successful Bake Sale having boxed up items on display will increase your return. It also makes it easy for you to transport and display the baked goods.

BAKED GOODS

Ask every parent on your team or at your school to donate at least one baked item. On the morning of your sale, ask parents to bring the goods to a specific location where you can load them up and transport them to the event location.

- What else to bring:

- School Brochures/flyers

- Cover the tables with paper or table cloths. This will make end of evening clean up easier. Don't forget to also put coverings on the display and head tables.

- Bring a small sifter and a container of icing sugar.

Make the tables look nice with the tablecloth. When you put the items up for display in the boxes, sprinkle a small amount of icing sugar over the top. This hint is especially effective for parents who didn't have time to bake something themselves and/or bought something. It just adds a little personal touch.

Unbelievably some people prefer store bought items.

Other things to remember:

Don't sell individual slices.
Sell full pies or cakes only.
Simplify prices.
One price for cakes, one for pies.
Once you sell out, you're done for the day

SOFT DRINKS AND BOTTLED WATER

Check with the business hosting your event if you can sell soft drinks and bottled water.

If they say it is fine, you can request donations of water and soft drinks.

If you get a lot of donations or choose to buy soft drinks and bottled water, you'll also need some ice – and coolers.

You'll also need to price the drinks so you're not losing money if you pay for them upfront.

If you receive donations or buy drinks in bulk, you can charge less – but keep in mind you're there to make a profit.

FUNDRAISING IDEAS

10.

LIQUOR LOCKER

This sounds like a strange idea, but it is actually a lot of fun.

To begin, ask parents to donate one or two bottles of any kind of liquor they have on hand. Unopened – it is understood but just in case...

You can also request donations from local restaurant, bars, pubs, etc.

At your event, wrap a chain link around all of the liquor - hence the name. You can box and wrap the locker up with gift-wrapping and a bow for effect.

You will need a lock on the front of the Liquor Locker.

Prior to the event, you will need to place a value upon the liquor locker. What would store value be for the all the accumulated bottles?

You then sell tickets during your event.

This was extremely popular at our Fundraising Events.

Remind people to purchase tickets at every possible opportunity.

After all of the tickets have been sold and at an allocated time, people with tickets will line up and each one will receive a key, but only one key will open the actual liquor locker.

It could be the first person in line or the last one, that's what is exciting about this event.

The winner takes the entire contents of the locker home.

FUNDRAISING IDEAS

11.

SILENT AUCTION

As discussed as a part of the Trivia Night Event earlier, this task will be a big money earner for you, but it takes a lot of organization.

You will need to choose the items from donated items and make a bidding sheet. Attendees will bid for items in increments chosen by you and listed on the bidding sheet in between rounds (while the judges are checking out the answers.)

The items should be displayed on the same table with the bidding sheets. Bidding sheets should include the item, value, and number of item and leave space for the person bidding to print their name, child's name and class, and bid. If not just for in house bidders, you should also add phone number to the form.

VALUABLE ITEMS

Valuable items, which could be carried off like gift certificates, should not be displayed - instead, an envelope stating what the gift certificate is for or a photocopy should be displayed - this is to avoid items going missing. Ask people to make bids between each round. Before the final round, ask for one last round of bids then collect the sheets. The winning bids can be tabulated and at the end of the evening people can claim their prizes and pay the winning amount.

Also make a list of all items up for grabs and put that list on each of the tables. Participants can choose which items they want to bid on before bidding opens and get excited about the items available.

(For full details refer back to Trivia Night Item #1.)

FUNDRAISING IDEAS

12.

AUCTION

I f you're game to add a full-on auction to your event, then first of all you will need an auctioneer or MC. Second you will need a place to hold your event. Then set your date and time and begin to ask for donations of items to auction off.

Some fundraising ideas for the auction:

- Auction off Deeds instead of items:

- Parents donate their time to assist other parents (like babysitting, grocery shopping, etc.)

- Parents donate their services to assist other parents (printing services, lawn mowing, etc.)

You can do a combination of the items above.
Be creative.

ALSO IMPORTANT:

Once you have everything in place, you need to prepare sheets for the auctioneer/MC to know what starting price you would like.

It would be worthwhile to prepare a master sheet which people will sign upon entry. They would give you their name, address, phone number and child's name and classroom. You could then give them an accompanying bidding number.

It would also be worthwhile to have auction items on display so bidders can look at the items before they bid.

If you have everything in place, collect the money and handing out the goods should be very straightforward. You can decide if you will accept only cash, or cheques or debit (you may need to source a card machine.)

FUNDRAISING IDEAS

13.

CRAPPY GIFTS!

We touched upon this fundraising idea under the Trivia Night Umbrella, but it's possible to make into a mini event of its own.

Ask parents, teachers, and the community to donate any unwanted and or nearly new items. We call them "Crappy Gifts."

Think of this idea as a remedy for clutter. Spring Cleaning for gifts you didn't want or need (or have any idea what they are for.)

It's worth mentioning again – to have fun with the theme. Don't be embarrassed if one of your gifts is donated to the Crappy Gift Table.

After all it's a way they can get rid of duplicates, or unwanted new or nearly latest items - all for a worthy cause. Nothing personal.

FUNDRAISING IDEAS

14.

POP A BALLOON PRIZES!

I f you have a lot of small prizes for a large event, an effective way to have fun with them is to put numbers inside a balloon and have people pop them.

They pay for the balloon and win the prize allocated to that number.

For this all you need are prizes and balloons.

If you have a lot of prizes it might be worthwhile to rent or invest in a balloon inflator or pump.

FUNDRAISING IDEAS

15.

COUNT THE JELLY BEANS (WITH A TWIST)

E veryone loves to guess how many jelly beans are in a jar.

We had success in having two jars, one for adults and one for the kids.

Prior to our event, we set up outside of the school and the children bid on the jelly bean jar.

At the Trivia Night, we had a jar full of chocolate covered coffee beans for the adults to guess how many.

You can use something else besides the coffee beans, as they can be a bit expensive. We had ours donated by a specialized wholesale retailer but these days, some grocery stores carry them.

Note: Ensure the lids are securely fastened. We had one adult open the jar to have a taste! This changed the count, but was easily managed.

FUNDRAISING IDEAS

16.

CHOCOLATE SALE

There are many established companies out there who buy chocolate bars in bulk and organize everything for you to sell chocolates (or other items) to the parents at your school, etc.

With these businesses, you are not keeping the entire profit, but they give you everything you need in order to have a successful fundraiser and as time is money this might suit your school or team.

Check on-line for options available near you.

Alternatively, if you have a local business who makes their own confectionary/chocolates you may be able to negotiate a partnership with them.

FUNDRAISING IDEAS

17.

WINE SALE!

This is another organized event, in which you sell bottles of wine.

It is all organized for you and the paperwork is given to you. You sell the wine and receive a percentage of the profits.

What you need to make sure that you do, is taste the wine, before you recommend it.

Request that a couple of complimentary bottles be sent to your team of volunteers before you begin selling.

This just helps you in case the wine isn't as good as you would like (or the parents would like.)

As a fundraiser it can work well, but only if customers are happy with the product itself.

This is an excellent idea for a birthday, new home, anniversary, Christmas, New Year's, or a gift for any occasion!

FUNDRAISING IDEAS

18.

HANDPRINTS

This is excellent if your child is in Preschool or Kindergarten and the teacher would like to work directly with your team of volunteers on this project.

The teacher would take handprints of each of the children in the class. The hands prints would then be labeled signed and up for sale.

Parents purchase them as a fundraiser for the classroom.

If a laminating machine is on hand (a good investment for schools and teams alike), copies can be made for Grandparents and other members of the family for an additional cost.

An unforgettable gift which can also be framed and passed down from generation to generation.

FUNDRAISING IDEAS

19.

GARDEN BULBS AND/OR SEEDS

This is another event, which you can probably find organizers for in your area.

Your school would sell in advance a variety of bulbs or seeds prior to planting season.

You would gain a profit from the sales, not the entire amount.

The bulbs would be delivered to the school for distribution.

Beautifying and creating a garden at your school can be a community builder and it can encourage parents and children to work together.

This could be a project in itself, where you could add-on other fundraising events like a Sausage/Hotdog Sizzle.

FUNDRAISING IDEAS

20.

CALENDARS!

Y ou may be able to find an outside firm to create a calendar for your school, again they would organize everything, and you would sell the calendars in advance.

You would ask for submissions of artwork from each of the classes or you could use class photographs.

If you are with a firm, they would give you the documentation required including forms and they would handle the money. You would then receive a cut of the profits from the orders made.

The completed calendars would be delivered to your school and distributed.

If you prefer to go for the DIY calendar and have an excellent printer, then you can put together a calendar with your team using some of the information above. The design and concept would be entirely yours and you could be more creative.

Alternatively, you would need to find a local printing company who could bind together the calendar for you.

If you don't have the budget, you could make a 1-page calendar for the entire year, including a photo or drawing created at the top of each calendar.

FUNDRAISING IDEAS

21.

JUMPING CASTLE!

These can be excellent if you are having an outdoor event, but you may need to check regarding licensing, insurance, and other rules in your specific municipality.

Many companies rent out Jumping Castles on commission, I.e., you would have no upfront costs but after the Jumping Castle rental amount has been covered, you would earn profits.

This could be a risky fundraising event if the weather is bad, and your event is outdoors.

Generally, not a promising idea if you aren't in a reliable climate.

NOTE: Insurance may not be covered even when the jumping castle is within your school or team's property. Ask the school or park if purchasing additional insurance is required in case of an accident.

FUNDRAISING IDEAS

22.

CAR PARKING VENUE

If your school was fortunate enough to be near a stadium, park, concert or other venues where the public gathers, then it would be a good idea to provide parking when it is needed (for a particular day or event.)

This would mean that you should be on the mailing list for any/all events, which could be coming up near you. It would mean a few parents would need to be on location to collect monies and to ensure the cars are safe while they attend the event. Also, after the event to ensure everyone gets out and away safely.

For this fundraiser, you have no overhead.

Best to plan on the weekends when the school is closed.

You may require additional insurance. Always check with your municipality, state, province prior to promoting your event.

FUNDRAISING IDEAS

23.

GALA DAY EVENT

A Gala Day is a huge event, which may encompass many of the above fundraising ideas.

You can select which ones will suit your special day.

It should be an outdoor event so weather will be a key factor in your success.

It should encompass a variety of games, events, food, and fun such as:

JUMPING CASTLES
FAIR RIDES
SPORTING ACTIVITIES
FLEA MARKET SALE
LIVE MUSIC.

Choose from these 103 Fundraising Ideas and put together your agenda for the day.

You may wish to include speakers, performers, etc., in which case a stage would be required, with chairs and perhaps even a tent overhead in case of harsh weather.

A sound system would add to festivities and draw people to your event.

A Gala Day can be an annual event.

Once you have a system in place and know what works and what doesn't.

FUNDRAISING IDEAS

24.

CHILDREN'S MOVIE NIGHT

This is a fundraiser where the school staff gets directly involved and the parents go out for a few hours.

Children dressed in their pajamas are dropped off at the school at an allotted time.

Children will be served pizza; soft drinks and they will watch pre-approved movies.

Note: check in advance no children have allergies.

Pre-booking will be required and an agreed upon fee per family would be collected in advance of the event.

Firm rules must be set in place.

For example:

Parents drop off children at 5 p.m.

Parents pick up children at 9 p.m.

The Principal and school staff will look after your children during the allotted hours. A menu should be agreed upon in advance, including beverages and the age-appropriate entertainment should be selected and promoted in advance.

The school would have contact names and numbers for all of the parents, in the event of a child becoming ill or a parent not picking up at the allotted time.

A good fundraiser with extremely low overhead.

It's an opportunity for the school or team leaders to say THANKS by giving the parents and volunteers a night off!

FUNDRAISING IDEAS

25.

CASINO NIGHT!

This night can be set up with a series of games of chance and gambling activities.

Suggested Casino Games:

Blackjack Table

Poker Table

Roulette Wheel.

If you have a budget, you could hire out some one arm bandits and have them set up for your event.

If budget is low, you could also incorporate some more Traditional Games:

Chess

Backgammon

Trivial Pursuit

Monopoly.

Note: you will probably need a gambling license (and a liquor license.)

Add some fun with:

Door Prizes
Raffles
Silent Auction.
If you have budget, you could cater the event, or make it BYO (BRING YOUR OWN.)

FUNDRAISING IDEAS

26.

SNAIL RACES!

For this fundraiser, you need to have some live snails. Depending on time of year, you might find them in your garden. Don't worry, they won't be harmed.

We attended a Salute To France Night –
They called it:

ESCARGOT LES COURSES.

Participants choose one of your snails.

A dot is placed on its shell – so you know which snail belongs to which contender.

Each snail is placed at the START LINE in a row.

SET A TIMER

At an allotted time begin the snail race.

Contestants are allowed to talk to their snail – but not to touch them.

First snail over the FINISH line wins.

The winning contestant receives a prize.

Snails are then returned safely to the garden.

See above for ways to get prize donations.

Always check with council regarding bylaws.

KEY TIP #15
Don't add this event to Trivia Night. Snails take a long time to move about – you don't want your event to go way over the allotted time since many parents will have hired a babysitter.

FUNDRAISING IDEAS

27.

MORNING OR AFTERNOON TEA OR COFFEE

This is a lovely social activity for parents and a good fundraiser.

Donations: sandwiches, cakes, cookies, teabags, and milk can all be requested as donations from parents.

Set up a room and set the table with with dainty cups and saucers. It's also nice to have table clothes and napkins. Parents from the school can donate all of these items too.

Charge an entry fee.

You can ask the Principal or some of the parents to speak.

Children can perform.

Mostly a social event for parents to get to know each other while raising money for the school at the same time.

WITH A TWIST

For a healthier option, make it a JUICE EVENT!

Donations: Parents with Juicers at home can bring them in and help with the event. A variety of fruits (and veggies) could be donated to create a variety of juices to taste. Or just choose a MENU of a few favourites. Cheese and crackers, or finger sandwiches could also be prepared or donated.

Then follow the instructions above.

FUNDRAISING IDEAS

28.

COIN TOSS/ROLL A COIN EVENT

This is a derivative of the Coin Roll.

People would toss a coin in the direction of a specific prize and whoever gets the closest wins the prize.

A bottle of champagne or other alcohol can be donated and also work well for this. For the little ones, a large stuffed animal would work well.

Always check with council regarding by-laws.

FUNDRAISING IDEAS

29.

COOKBOOKS!

There are many organizations that can assist you with this as a fundraiser. A classroom or school would ask for recipes to be donated to form into a book. People would then order the books, and a portion of the profits would go to the school.

Paperwork would be given to you as well as deadlines, which must be strictly adhered to.

Little to no overhead involved if you use one of the companies who specialize in this area.

DO IT YOURSELF

PRINTING

Can be awfully expensive if you go it alone.

Alternatively, if you had a good printer and access to a good graphic artist in your committee or group and lots of spare time - you could put together the book yourself.

A local printer or photo copying company might be able to assist you in your venture.

eBook

If print is too difficult, you could design and create an eBook Cookbook. There are several programs on-line to assist you.

FUNDRAISING IDEAS

30.

CREATE YOUR OWN WINE LABEL!

This is another organized event, in which you sell bottles of wine.

However, with this one, the main selling point is that the wine labels will reflect the logo of your school or team.

This would require you to have a logo, which the company can use to create a suitable label, but otherwise things would go pretty much the same as for selling wine above.

Alternatively, your group works with a local DIY wine cellar and creates your own wine and branding.

As mentioned above, it is especially important to test the wine before you let the company put your school or team logo on it.

FUNDRAISING IDEAS

31.

CHESS TOURNAMENTS!

I f you have a few chess champions in your midst, then this could be a fun morning or afternoon fundraiser.

Ask families if they are able to donate their Chess Boards for the events. Make sure you label them and return them in the same condition as received.

You could sell tickets to view the Chess Tournaments.

You would need prizes for the winner of the tournament and perhaps also for the runner up player.

You can seek donations as per instructions above.

You could buy food and soft drinks and sell them (or ask for donations of these items.)

You would need an MC or someone to ensure the auditorium was quiet and to keep the players moving and the time limits adhered to.

An alarmed time clock would be beneficial.

Always check with your municipality or council regarding bylaws.

FUNDRAISING IDEAS

32.

SPELLING BEE!

If you are interested in involving the children and creating an event the Spelling Bee could be a good option. Since you have the facility and a contact list, all you would need was an apparatus to narrow down the children who would participate from each class. The Principal could be the M.C. This could also be an excellent way to meet potential new students and for parents to network.

You can use some of the methods mentioned above in order to get donations of prizes.

You could also ask for donations for food and drink or buy and sell this as a part of the fundraiser. You could also do a Sausage/Hot Dog Sizzle.

See above for ideas to top off and maximize your fundraising results.

FUNDRAISING IDEAS

33.

GUESS THAT SONG MUSIC NIGHT!

This would be a version of an old television show which has recently been revised called: "Name That Tune."

As with the Trivia Night, you would ask people to form groups, and teams. You would also require an MC.

Alternatively, you could hire a DJ, or you could organize a themed playlist. These could easily be played via a computer or a sound system.

The purpose of the game would be for the teams to guess what lyrics came next or what the song title was, what album it came from, what year it was released in or who the singer/band was.

You can use some of the game options from the above event suggestions.

I would suggest that you choose which elements from Trivia Night you would like to include in order to maximize your fundraising results.

Selling tickets in advance for this event would bring in the maximum amount of funds.

If you already have two major events for the year, you may wish to make this a secondary event. In which case it's best if you don't overcomplicate it.

FUNDRAISING IDEAS

34.

GIFT HAMPERS!

There are many organizations that prepare Gift Hampers as fundraisers and pay you a portion of the profits. Check on-line to see which type of Hamper you think would be the best seller and what time of year would suit your fundraiser.

By using an organization to put everything together for you, it should be relatively easy and there should be exceptionally low overhead.

Once they send you the flyers with costs for the hampers, you send copies to the parents and they order accordingly.

DO IT YOURSELF

But you don't have to go with an outside organization.

This can be a Do-it-yourself project, where you ask for donations from local businesses and create your gift hampers. You would then create your own flyers and/or have an event day when people could purchase your Gift Hampers.

If you tie them in with a specific day or event or theme this could really boost your sales.

Example:

Valentine's Day Hampers

Christmas Hampers

March Break Hampers.

FUNDRAISING IDEAS

35.

GREETING CARDS!

Another favourite fundraiser, which can be organized via companies who specialize in this area. Check on-line for the one that suits. Generally, a package of cards, which can be used for every occasion, is the most popular one to invest in.

As with other organized fundraisers you would receive a portion of the profits, and everything is pretty much organized for you.

Note: Try not to have too many of these fundraisers during the year. Parents are on budgets, and surprising them with new events all the time will not go down well.

Choose a couple of events, which you think will go over well. Listen to feedback. Don't over fundraise and upset parents.

Try to branch out and fundraise from other sources too.

FUNDRAISING IDEAS

36.

COOKIE DRIVE!

Another excellent fundraiser, which is, pretty much organized for you. All you have to do is find the fundraising company with the right fit for your school and to sign up. They will give you everything to need to ensure a successful campaign.

As above your school/team will receive a portion of the profits.

Again, your committee could do a cookie-baking weekend and box and sell the cookies you made yourselves. This is an excellent opportunity to get people together and to create a stronger sense of purpose and community.

Add coffee and it could be quite a lucrative fundraiser.

Don't forget to check with your local council or municipality regarding food handling or other licenses which may be required.

FUNDRAISING IDEAS

37.

HEADS AND TAILS!

We touched upon this game as a part of Trivia Night, but it can be a very successful and fun option on any event night.

Place an empty bowl on each of the tables.

The MC should explain how the game will work.

Team members will each throw $1.00 coin into the bowl.

The Master of Ceremonies will ask questions and participants choose whether the answer is a Head or Tails answer.

The last person standing will be the winner.

They will receive a prize.

Ensure that monies are collected from the table by one of your team members immediately after each individual game is played. This will ensure that the bowls are empty for forthcoming games.

All of the monies earned should be brought to one person who is responsible for the safe keeping of the funds during the evening.

FUNDRAISING IDEAS

38.

SCRATCHIE LOTTERY CHRISTMAS TREE!

We touched upon this as an element of Trivia Night, but this game can be an excellent standalone fundraiser or a part of any fundraising event. When the weather changes, use the appropriate tree for the season!

In your school newsletter, ask parents to donate scratchie lottery tickets (one or more.) Tell them about the Scratchie Tree and the event, which they will be able to bid and perhaps win all the tickets.

Visit local lottery ticket sellers, corner stores, etc., with the letter about your event and ask for donations for the Scratchie Tree. You'll be surprised at how many businesses will donate one or two tickets.

You can choose whether to make this a Silent Auction or Auction item at your event.

If you hold this as an Auction item later in the evening at your event, you will probably make the most money for your fundraiser.

Building the Scratchie Tree

Drawn an outline of a tree. If you have someone who is a little bit artistic, they can create a piece of art. If not, a simple outline of a tree will still work.

Use masking tape (not glue) and place the tickets onto the tree one by one.

A Real Tree

We had a donation of a plastic tree to our fundraiser. We were able to use masking tape to place the tickets onto the branches and it looked quite amazing.

The winner won the tree itself and the tickets.

Feel free to improvise.

FUNDRAISING IDEAS

39.

WHO DONE IT MURDER MYSTERY EVENT!

There are many organizations that will put together a Mystery or Whodunit Evening for you. Some will have their own facility, and some will come to you. You will need to work out how you will raise funds from attendance.

The best thing about this is you will have a professional company organizing everything and it will ensure an excellent event.

See how you can incorporate some of the fundraising games listed here during the night to maximize your fundraising experience.

If you want to, you could manage this fundraiser as a DIY event. All you need is imagination. Find out more about these events on-line and create your own fundraiser.

Don't forget to check with your local council or municipality for any bylaws.

FUNDRAISING IDEAS

40.

FACTORY OUTLET SHOPPING TOUR!

Who doesn't love Shopping? Especially coming into the busy Christmas period.

There are many companies who will organize everything for you, including the bus to take you from Factory Outlet to Factory Outlet and to keep you on track and maximize the amount of shopping and spending for your group.

Once you find the company who visits the variety of outlets you think you can sell to parents and friends of your school or team, they will give you all of the information which will help you sign people up and to ensure a successful event.

Keep in mind that they usually have a minimum amount of people who need to be enrolled in order for your Shopping Tour to be worthwhile.

Your school/team will be paid a percent of the profits from all the money spent.

Note: the Factory Outlets visited by your school or team often donate items to your bus tour based upon how much you spend in their store. These items can be prizes for your guests and a good incentive to get involved in your Shopping Tour.

This is an excellent, fun way to raise funds. Once a year is usually enough for this event.

FUNDRAISING IDEAS

41.

TEA TOWELS!

This is an excellent fundraiser, especially when your children first start school.

There are companies, which organize everything for you so you can fundraise and collect the most amounts of monies.

At Your School

The teachers will be requested to ask each child in their class to draw a portrait of themselves, or make a handprint. Then sign their name beside it. All of these drawings will then be incorporated onto a tea towel with the school logo and year.

Families buy lots of these as gifts for grandparents, uncles, and aunts, etc.

Your school will be paid a portion from the profits.

FUNDRAISING IDEAS

42.

TEMPORARY TATTOOS AND FACE PAINTING!

Stick on tattoos are a lot of fun and no risk.

You can ask for donations or buy quite a lot of temporary tattoos for a small amount of money.

Children will line up to receive a temporary tattoo of their favorite movie or cartoon character.

This is a low overhead cost, but due to demand you may wish to have 3 or 4 volunteers to apply the tattoos.

Charge a minimal amount for each tattoo.

With Face Painting, it is often fairly easy to find parents who will volunteer to paint the children's faces as part of a fundraiser and who have access to a kit.

If not, you may have to hire a professional face painter for your event and work out a percentage, which will be taken from the profits.

These two elements go hand in hand and for any all-day event will draw in families and make parents and children alike incredibly happy.

FUNDRAISING IDEAS

43.

FASHION SHOW!

As a fundraiser, a fashion show can be a complex event if you don't have access to:

- A Stage/Runway

- A Designer

- A Designer's Clothes

- Models

- An MC

- Photographer

- Music.

The first item on the list can be created with a stage and with adding a platform on the front so the models can walk among the audience.

Check on costs before you go any further and work out details about insurance, access to your building, rental, installation, and pickup after your event before you move on to Step 2.

If you know an up-and-coming designer in your area who would like to get some exposure for his/her line, then this could work out well.

If not, you may wish to link up with a local fashion store or you may find a related source on-line.

Your fundraiser will be based upon selling donated outfits or receiving a percentage from sales of clothes from your fashion show.

If you don't have access to a Designer, then do not move on to Step 3.

If you have access to a Designer, he/she will more than likely be able to put you in touch with some models. If there is a local modeling school, you may be able to request volunteers for your event in return for exposure. Modeling Agencies may be able to assist you and if you are lucky, they might send a few volunteers your way. If not, hiring models could become very costly.

If you have all three of the above steps in place, then you can choose a night for your event and make sure everything is in place above for the specific night and time.

Now you need an M.C. - who will be able to describe (read descriptions) of the models, keeping the evening moving and on track. The MC would also describe what the models are wearing, to entertain the audience while the models are changing, and to keep up the pace with a busy auction.

What would a fashion night be without a Photographer? Get a volunteer to take photos during the night.

Sound System. In addition to the microphone for the MC, you'll also need music. Use a playlist on your phone or laptop with speakers. It's all down to budget.

SPONSORSHIP

For an event as large as this, you may wish to approach a few businesses for sponsorship. You an offer them signage at the event, social media exposure and a Certificate of Appreciation after the event. Be careful whom you choose for sponsorship, as you don't want any conflicts with your Designer.

Send out invitations to media to come along and cover your event.

Check if wine, beer, and food can be sold at your event location. If yes, you can charge a higher price for entry. I would also recommend you ask for donations of prizes. Please follow the instructions above from Trivia Night.

If the Designer agrees to donate several outfits, these can be bid upon at an Auction while the models are on the runway.

Note: audience members may not be the size of the model on the runway. Talk to the Designer about this beforehand. If he/she is willing to create the outfit to size for the winning bidder, then it will increase your overall results. If you are working with a local store, they will be able to tell you which sizes they have available.

Don't forget to check with your municipality about licenses and insurance.

This is a large event which will take maximum amount of planning, but results will be well worth it if everything is managed and your event is presented in a format which will be well regarded.

Once you have a system for your event, the next one will be easier.

ON SALE DAY

Expect people to make an offer. Be willing to negotiate. You do not want to put all the unsold goods into storage for the next sale. However, don't go too low after all the work you put into this you will want to achieve the best results.

Note: you will have hangers-on people, those who hang around until the sale is just about finished and want to get a rock bottom price for an item. Decide if you could sell it when you hold the event again, if not get rid of it for whatever you can get for it.

Check with council about permits or licenses for your event. Add elements from the suggestions above. The more events you have onsite the longer people will hang around.

If you wish, you could sell plots for others to sell their items too.

See Car Boot Sale 103 Fundraising Idea #44!

FUNDRAISING IDEAS

44.

CAR BOOT (OR TRUNK) SALE!

This is like a community garage sale but instead of allocating spaces, the people sell from the trunk (or boot) of their car. Saturdays and Sundays are best days for Car Boot Sales. Advertise your event in local newspapers, online community websites and ask people if they want to buy a stall.

Price items reasonably and you will sell out in no time.

As an organizer of this event, you sell spaces in advance as you have a limited amount of space.

Check if any permits or licenses are required before you begin.

If you would prefer not to have vehicles all over the school property, then the sale could be in the parking lot. If the parking lot isn't a big enough size to make this worthwhile, then I suggest you allocate plots of land. You can then sell a small size and a generous size.

Your sellers will do their own setting up; you can indicate spaces with masking tape or by using chalk on the pavement. The sellers provide their own change and look after their own items, both setting up and You should have volunteers on site to assist in case you are needed.

It would be helpful to have washrooms available on site if possible, for the sellers if this is an all-day event.

To raise additional funds and to draw people in, a Sausage or Hotdog Sizzle is highly recommended. You can add other child friendly elements from the list above if you wish.

FUNDRAISING IDEAS

45.

WHITE ELEPHANT SALE!

A White Elephant Sale is like a giant community garage sale - without the garage.

Due to its large proponent for a dependency on donations, it is best to have this event every two or three years.

For this event, you ask parents and friends to donate items, which they no longer need or don't use anymore. Things, which often they would donate to charities or throw, away, they will save and give you the school or team as a fundraiser.

The first thing you are going to need is STORAGE. I mean massive storage. You will get everything from treadmills to cribs to sinks to toys. Lots of toys and stuffed animals. If your school can allocate storage to you, then I'd say go ahead with this event.

Unless you have a massive garage with nothing in it, just waiting to be filled up, I would suggest it be kept on the school grounds just needing to be sorted and ready for the sale.

Keep in mind, if you move it off-site then you will need to transport it back and trust me you will get a lot of donations.

Put up signs around the school and in the newsletter requesting goods to be donated for your White Elephant Sale. Ask for donations to be dropped off at specific times Before School and After School work well. You don't want the dropping off of items to interfere with the school curriculum or to interfere with staff and/or daily schedules. You will need to have members of your team available to move the items into storage. This can be a fun job for volunteers as they get to see donations first. Make it a rule no one can buy items before the actual sale day.

It can be handy to put together a list of items as you go collecting them, or, if you prefer you can organize it the day prior.

Assess and reassess.

If you have a thousand items to get through on the day before you will need a lot of helpers.

Once you have the items, you will need to price them. This can be done by buying stickers and tagging each item or by creating specific areas for items, which are managed by a team of one or two persons.

FUNDRAISING IDEAS

46.

FLEA MARKET!

With a Flea Market, your scope is somewhat larger than a Car Boot Sale or Garage Sale. You can sell to professional retailers and have a large variety of items up for sale.

With this again, you would need to check with local council regarding licenses and insurance.

You could advertise in local newspapers and online community events columns for retailers or people who would like to sell their handmade goods. You can offer several varieties of sizes for booths, but the retailers will be responsible for setup, takedown and sales/cash for their items.

You will need to have staff on-site and you will need a large area for a Flea Market where there can be quite a bit of traffic (walking and parking.) Check with local council to see if they may have something in a central location which they would donate or reduce cost to you for your fundraising event.

If you wish, you can add elements from above including your own school or team marketing stall. The more elements you add the more money you will make, but the more complicated the task becomes.

FUNDRAISING IDEAS

47.

BARE FOOT BOWLING!

This is Lawn Bowling with a fun name. Contact your local Lawn Bowling Facility and ask if they rent out the facility for fundraising events. Check to see if they will donate the space to your event for free or at a reduced cost.

If the Lawn Bowling Facility has lights, an enjoyable time to have your event is in the evening so as not to disrupt their regular clientele.

Ask if they could open up their kiosk and organize someone to look after it, and give you a percentage of profits from the sales or if they are donating the facility to your event and are non-profit themselves, they could also raise funds for their facility. They might even know a local band and/or singer who'd like to help. Win Win.

After choosing a date and time, include information in your school's newsletter about your event. Sell tickets for families.

Seek out donations for prizes. Look back at Trivia Night suggestions.

Shoes are of course taken off and all bowlers bowl barefooted. It's more fun this way for the entire family.

Add elements like face painting, removable tattoos if the facility permits.

Don't forget to check with council in case permits or licenses are required.

FUNDRAISING IDEAS

48.

BOWLING ANYONE?

S traight up bowling at your local facility.

You would need to negotiate a take-over of the entire facility on a particular day as a fundraising event.

You would bring in the bowlers for an agreed upon fee (including dinner or snacks if the facility has them) and your school will take a percentage from total sales.

If you have a community minded Bowling Lane and they are on board, this should be a relatively easy sell for families at your school or in your team with little to no overhead. Bonus would be lots of parking available on site.

Check with local council in case permits or licenses or insurance are required.

FUNDRAISING IDEAS

49.

IDOL SEARCH!

M any stars can be discovered when your community has a local idol search - including Justin Bieber.

To set up your own event for your school, you would need to ask for volunteers, singers and groups who would be interested in performing in public in order to win the title of *Name of Your School or Team Goes Here* Idol. You can charge an entry fee if you wish.

Once you have a date and a venue, you will need a band that will volunteer their time for the evening (or who you can pay) and/or a karaoke machine.

The latter will still work and then people who get a little stage fright don't have to be worried about forgetting the words (unlike what usually happens on the TV show.)

Send out letters and request donations for prizes (see Trivia Night prize information above.)

You should ask a parent to be the MC, or the Principal or Coach might wish to take on this role.

A microphone will be needed.

JUDGES

You will require a minimum of 3 judges. They can rate the performances, or you can use audience applause as a gauge.

You will need plenty of chairs if you don't already have them on hand, check with a local hall or another nearby school to see if you could borrow theirs. Either way, you will have to ask parents to assist or have a truck transport chairs.

FOOD & DRINKS

You can choose to sell soft drinks, food, etc., if you wish and ask for donations or buy these items. You will need someone on hand to man this booth and collect the monies.

A floater of change should be available and recorded to be reimbursed after the event.

RECORDING

If you are able to, have someone professionally video tape the event. Parents will line up for a good copy of their child singing. You can make these available on DVD for a nominal fee.

As per usual, check with council regarding additional licenses or insurance which might be required.

FUNDRAISING IDEAS

50.

TALENT SEARCH!

This fundraiser is Idol Search but on a much larger scale as you will be asking for Contestants to enter and win a prize from outside of your school or team.

For this event, you will need a larger hall with a stage and a bigger sound system. Most large facilities will have plenty of chairs on hand, if not you will have to rent them or bring them in. Some suggestions on how to do this can be found under the Idol Search tab. You may want to check into this and see what options are available before you go any further.

I would also recommend checking to see what licenses, insurance or permits would be necessary.

Once you have all the above, choose a date.

Start promoting via free avenues such as social media, local newspapers, online events calendars. Contact local radio stations too as this is music related and radio stations are generally very community-minded they might want to be involved as a sponsor.

You could also ask a local celebrity from the station to MC the event or to be one of the judges. You should have two or three judges in total for the event.

For music, you could hire a local band, or you could go the karaoke route. Up to you how you want to network in your area.

ENTRY FEE

Choose a suitable entry fee for participants and request payment in advance.

Now, start asking for donations of prizes and start to sell tickets to your event.

Decide if you want to have any fundraising games from this list while the judges are deliberating.

If you can get most things donated, then you can keep your overhead relatively low.

FUNDRAISING IDEAS

51.

COMEDY CLUB NIGHT OUT

A combination of the Idol Search and Talent Search but specific to the comedic category.

If you open this up to the general public, you might want to be in a facility where alcohol and food are being sold in order to maximize the scope for your fundraiser.

Follow the above steps from the last two fundraising events in order to get publicity, an MC, and judges.

You may be able to work directly with a facility, which runs these events regularly, and take in a portion of the profits. Better prizes will draw in more contestants. Don't forget to charge a good entry fee.

Also, it is recommended that you warn attendees that content is 18+.

Don't forget to check with council to see if any insurance, licenses, etc., are required.

FUNDRAISING IDEAS

52.

GAMES DAY!

First you need to decide what kind of games you would like to include. Would you like your Games Day to be an Outdoor or Indoor Event? You should check either way whether you will need licenses or permits from local council or municipality.

OUTDOOR GAMES

You could set up an Olympic-Like track and invite children at your school to compete for ribbons. However, you don't have to include real Olympic games.

Some suggestions:
- Biggest Bubble-gum Bubble

- Relay Race

- Fastest Popcorn Eater

- Spoon and Egg Race

- Three-Legged Race

Use your imagination. Make of list of things you will need and ask for donations for prizes. Create teams of children.

Invite the parents to come along and have food and drinks for sale. You can add other elements from the list above if you want to fundraise on a larger scale.

Back Up Plan Incase It Rains...Set a rain date.

INDOOR GAMES FOR PARENTS

Set up a variety of board games such as Trivial Pursuit, Chess, The Game of Life, Charades, etc.

This can be an all-adult event where people move from table to table or game to game.

Winner gets the most points at the end of the evening.

You might be able to make it a BYO Wine event where you sell wine glasses. You might wish to include food. Ask for donations for all the above.

The scale on which you choose to do the bottom fundraiser is up to you.

This could even be done as a fundraiser out of a home when inviting some friends.

If multiple families held such an event as a fundraiser in their homes and charged an entry fee this could be a good little fundraiser with little overhead.

FUNDRAISING IDEAS

53.

FUN RUN!

This event can be as simple or as complex as you wish it to be, but my advice is to keep it simple if you are fundraising for a school or a team.

After choosing the route and distance of your event, you will need to clear it with council in regard to insurance, registration, or any other necessary permits. This will be especially important if you are using any streets or places with public access like parks.

Alternatively, you can create a route and distance within the grounds of your school. All you need are chalk lines or pylons to mark the space.

Choose a time and date for your event and create a sponsor sheet to send home with students or team members. The sponsor sheet should indicate distance or time which the student or team member can be sponsored.

You may wish to include a letter, or a paragraph indicating why you are having a Fun Run and what the money is required for. Also indicate that the children will have the opportunity to win prizes and it will be a fun day for the entire family. If you divide the children into smaller teams, you may wish to ask them to wear a certain colour on the event day. Having a team event and prizes will make it more fun for all.

You will need to buy ribbons - for 1st, 2nd and 3rd prizes. I would recommend prizes for teams, too. You should request donations for these from local businesses.

You may wish to incorporate other fundraising ideas from this list like the Sausage/Hotdog Sizzle, or to sell soft drinks. See if you can get bottles of water donated, as the runners will need plenty of it on hand.

After the event, collect the monies from the sponsors and thank all of those who gave donations with a Certificate of Appreciation.

FUNDRAISING IDEAS

54.

ASK FOR DONATIONS!

Need money? Need donations?

Quite simply, **ask for it** straight out.

Send a letter or email, telling parents what is required and asking them to contribute.

Fundraising requires a lot of time - and a lot of helping hands.

Often times you end up finding fun ways to get the parents and family involved - and so this is way of saying, this will be our only fundraiser this year and we need such and an amount from each of the parents this year.

If we meet our fundraising goals for this year, then no additional fundraising (or volunteering) will be required this year.

Straight up and effective.

You'll be amazed what unexpected events occur when you JUST ASK!

FUNDRAISING IDEAS

55.

PICNIC FUN DAY!

Families would be asked to prepare a PICNIC BASKET. These would be auctioned off.

Once all the picnic baskets have been won, everyone can indulge.

Note: with allergies this could complicate things so keep it in mind.

It can be difficult to make money from an event such as this without adding elements of fundraising such as Jumping Castles, Face Painting, Removable Tattoos, etc.

The basic idea though, is to get everyone together from your school or team to share food in an outdoor setting (weather permitted) and to network.

Events like this encourage involvement and friendship and are fun for everyone involved, however a little fundraising on the side can be an added bonus.

FUNDRAISING IDEAS

56.

SPORTS DAY!

A sport day is similar to a Games Day, but you might want to zero in on whatever sport is seasonally popular at the time.

The children can wear their uniforms and compete in small games; the winning team moves on to the next round.

You can seek prizes and sponsorships if you wish, but you should definitely have prizes (or ribbons) for the winning teams.

You can organize other fundraising elements like a BBQ (Sausage Sizzle/Hot Dog Sizzle), sell soft drinks, baked goods.

Always check in case there are licenses, insurance or other permissions required from local council.

FUNDRAISING IDEAS

57.

CAR WASHING EVENT!

This is a fairly easy event to organize; all you need are buckets of water, soap, shammies, sponges and lots of volunteers.

However, to maximize your fundraising day, it will all be down to

LOCATION. LOCATION.

Approach a busy location like a grocery store and ask if you can set one up in an area within their parking lot.

Even if they give you permission, you will still need to check to see if specific licenses or insurances are required from council. You may also need to get some Pylons to block off your area and to keep your volunteers safe.

If you have a volunteer (or two) who is willing to dress in a costume with a sign or sandwich board and flag down potential customers, this is an excellent way to attract strangers to your car-washing event.

Also promote internally to your school or team via emails and newsletters.

Contact local newspapers and radio stations telling about your event.

Start up an Event Page on Facebook and Twitter.

Post your event on local calendars. Make sure signage is clear about costs.

Make sure you have a floater so you can make change and indicate cash only unless you have access to credit/debit card machines.

UPDATE: INSURANCE

Most suitable locations for this event would have insurance – but will it cover your event?

If your can run the event on school property, it's easy to ensure you have the correct insurance policy in place since all student activities would be covered. Check though that coverage is extended for non-school hour events.

If you're at a grocery store it would be worth it to look into purchasing Event Insurance. Check with the manager to ensure that your school/team would be covered in the event of someone slipping.

When you contact your insurance, provider tell them you are holding a Car Wash Fundraising Event. They will best advise you on what is required.

FUNDRAISING IDEAS

58.

GOLF TOURNAMENT

P lanning is key to a successful golf tournament, and you will have to reserve your date with your local golf course way in advance for your fundraising event. An alternative might be to go smaller by fundraising with a Mini Golf Course. Check to see what options are available in your area and don't forget to ask about permits, licenses, and fees with local council.

Once you have the date and time locked in, start asking for Sponsors. For a Golf Tournament at a local and well-known Country Club you will be able to go for the large sponsors like car dealerships, local media, etc. You may want to have a classification of sponsors like Gold, Silver and Bronze and you will definitely want to go for large scale prizes. Some Golf Tournaments even give away a car.

Having a website will be key to your event. Again, this is going large scale, and you will need a lot of volunteers and resources in order to pull it off.

Charge a Registration Fee for Golfers. Make sure you include all items, which will be covered for the fee for example: Clubs, Day of Golfing, Cart, Food (Lunch? Dinner?), T-shirts, hats, alcohol, Silent Auction, Raffles, Door Prizes, etc.

Your event should include lots of prizes and opportunities to raise more funds through add-ons like a Silent Auction and Raffles. You need to request donations in addition to sponsors (scroll back to the Trivia Night Fundraising Event for helpful hints.)

FUNDRAISING IDEAS

59.

TREASURE HUNT!

This could easily be an after-school fundraiser, or if you want to make a full day of it that's possible too. Recommended you use the school grounds or a nearby park area once you check with council regarding permissions, licenses, etc. Costumes could be included with a prize for best Pirate!

For the Treasure Hunt itself, you may be able to charge an entry fee if you are keeping it within your school or team. If you were going to go for a larger fundraiser where you allow outside team and have really large prizes, then definitely an entry fee would be recommended.

Promote via the usual avenues once you have dates and bring some major sponsors on board using the tools available above for Trivia Night. Create a social media promotion and contact local media.

Once you have collected a wide variety of prizes, you should plan out a map and put together clues along the way.

The Winning team (or individual) would receive a prize. You might want to also give a prize for the Runner's Up.

After the Treasure Hunt, you may wish to incorporate other elements like a Sausage/Hotdog Sizzle and to sell soft drinks, etc.

FUNDRAISING IDEAS

60.

GUESS WHO? BABY PHOTO CONTEST!

This is strictly an in-house fundraiser.

You ask all of the children in your school or on your team to bring in baby photos and you post them on a large board with THEN and NOW photos, but you don't keep them together - you scramble them up.

The event can be in the evening or afternoon and you can incorporate food (whether it be finger foods or something more elaborate is up to you) and beverages including wine or soft drinks depending upon permissions and licenses from council and what your fundraising goals are.

Parents would pay an entry fee for the evening, and you can add in other games from the list above in order to make a night of it.

You will need donations for prizes, and you might be able to get sponsorship for your event from a local business.

A good fit would be a camera, photography, or phone) related business and they could donate the 1st prize.

You would need to put together a numbered list of the Then photos on the board.

You would need to put together an alphabetical list of the photos on the board for the NOWS. Leave paper and pens or pencils on each of the tables. Ask people to match up the THEN and NOWS with numbers and alphabets.

The winner would match the most correct photos from the Then and Now boards.

You may also wish to give a prize to the person got the most incorrect.

FUNDRAISING IDEAS

61.

WHO'S RELATED? BABY/PARENT CONTEST!

T his is an extension of the previous fundraiser, and you could use with fundraising idea #60 or it could stand alone as its own event.

The difference is - you have a baby photo of the child and a photo of one of the parents as a baby.

Participants must match up baby and parent photos.

All the other elements from #60 fundraising idea can be incorporated here.

FUNDRAISING IDEAS

62.

CHRISTMAS CRAFT STALL!

When Christmas is coming, we all tend to get a little creative and crafty and this is a way to use your artistic talents for fundraising purposes.

After choosing a date and time for your event, ask parents to start coming up with craft ideas and to make donations to your fundraiser.

It's true that parents will be spending money, and some will even buy back their own items from the stall. It is good if there is a local event in your city in which you can participate, or you can just hold your event at your school.

If you can ask the teachers to get the children to create crafts in class - parents will also buy these.

It's also good to add in other events from the list, I'll leave it to you how big you want your fundraiser to be.

Don't forget to check with council in case permits or licenses are required.

"Peace on earth will come to stay, when we live Christmas every day."

Helen Steiner Rice

FUNDRAISING IDEAS

63.

VALENTINE'S DAY STALL EVENT!

After you have chosen the day for your event, ask parents to make donations and you'll be amazed what comes in. As with some of the above ideas, you may need a space to store everything before your sale. If you don't have this, then I would suggest you move on to another idea.

It is good to incorporate a Bake Sale in with this event and also ask parents for donations of food items. Refer to suggestion # 9 for ideas.

As always check with council about licenses, permits, insurance, etc. beforehand.

You will need to price everything in advance and a floater is recommended.

Keeping this as an in-school or teamed event isn't as profitable but it keeps your overhead low and the children enjoy shopping and the day. For Mother's Day or Father's Day, the children are looking for a gift to give and if you tell the parents in advance of your stall then they will send the children to school with some money.

This type of stall can be used for whatever name day you prefer with low overhead and not a lot of work involved if you keep it internal to your group.

FUNDRAISING IDEAS

64.

MOTHER'S DAY GIFT STALL EVENT!

Sell inexpensive items every Mom would love to receive!

We asked parents to donate (or re-gift) items unopened items and were amazed what came in.

For parents who didn't have anything to donate, we suggested an inexpensive gift from a dollar store.

Some parents donated a bunch of flowers from a local florist.

Some donated homemade gifts like scarves, hats, baskets, or something crafty.

A note was sent home about the Mother's Day Gift Stall Event Day asking parents to send along a little pocket money with their child on the day to purchase a gift for their Mom.

SALE DAY

Children can "shop" for Mom and experience the joy of giving something they chose themselves.

A fun heart felt event for all.

FUNDRAISING IDEAS

65.

FATHER'S DAY GIFT STALL EVENT!

This is an extension of Fundraising Idea #64 For Father's Day.

For Father's we didn't ask for donations from home from the children.

Instead, we were able to acquire donations from a local retail men's wear store of socks and ties, in addition to some sports related memorabilia from a local shop.

We topped up these donations with gift bags we made ourselves from donated food items.

We sent a note home to parents about the Father's Day Gift Stall Event, as we did with the Mother's Day Event, so children could shop for their Dad's and choose a gift.

The Mother's Day and Father's Day Events could be combined, or a general Parent Day Event would also work using the same format.

FUNDRAISING IDEAS

66.

HALLOWEEN PARTY!

M any parents are concerned about children going out trick or treating and instead prefer their children to be involved in a Halloween Party so why not make it into a Fundraiser for your school or team?

I would not recommend charging an entry fee, however, if you would like to add in some other items like Movie Night or Game Night then perhaps a fee would be appropriate.

Check what licenses and permits council might require before you start to make plans.

Once you have alerted the parents to the date and time of your event by using social media or other tools like a newsletter or email, you can start to get donations for prizes. You will need prizes for Best Costume, Most Creative Costume, Scariest Costume, etc., depending on how many donations come in.

Go with Halloween related games like Dunking for Apples, Bingo, Pin the Tail on the Donkey (use something Halloween themed), Pop a Balloon, etc. You can be as creative as you want.

You may wish to ask parents to bake healthier theme related treats, but the night would be perfect without giving out some candy or gift bags.

FUNDRAISING IDEAS

67.

BIRTHDAY PARTY!

This can be a fundraiser if instead of asking for presents, your child chooses to ask for donations toward raising funds for their school or team.

On a larger scale, you could have a Birthday Party for your school or team and request donations for something specific which parents and families would be happy for the students/team to have.

Instead of money, you could request new books for the library as a birthday present to the school.

Be creative.

Note: Reward the Birthday Child with a Certificate of Thanks!

FUNDRAISING IDEAS

68.

BOOK SALE!

This can be a gargantuan task, just warning, because if you ask for books you will get a lot of donations and you will need to have space to store them. You will also need to be able to go through them individually and price them - and in order to do this correctly you will need to check (especially with older books, signed books and first edition books) how they should be priced. If you don't care what the book is worth - that makes your task easier, but you will still need a lot of storage.

You will also need a way to display the books so that people can buy them. I would suggest dividing the books into categories as they come in - this will save you a lot of headaches in the long run. They you can easily sell them in categories like:

- CHILDREN'S BOOKS

- COMICS/GRAPHIC NOVELS

- FICTION PAPERBACK

- FICTION HARD COVER

- NON-FICTION PAPERBACK

- NON-FICTION HARD COVER.

Book buyers don't mind sorting through, in fact they enjoy it, but the more organized your fundraising event is, the more you will sell (and you won't want to have to pack up leftovers and put them away into storage until next year's sale.)

Make sure you check for licenses, permits, etc., from local council.

Include any other fundraising elements from this list you wish.

Ask for donations of prizes, or sponsors if you wish.

FUNDRAISING IDEAS

69.

ANTIQUE FAIR!

A ntiques can be a bit tricky to price, so you might want to rent booths out to the professionals if you want to hold an Antique Fair.

After you have chosen your date and location and checked with council about permits, licenses, etc., you can start to promote via social media, newspapers, radio, and other local venues that you are looking for Antique Dealers.

This is pretty easy; you just request a fee for the booth space you are allotting.

Most antique dealers will have their own "system" for how they want to set up and display their goods. Most will even bring their own tables and chairs for the day. Be clear with the sellers that they are responsible for the method of payment for their booths and for having proper change, etc.

If you are having your event on school or team property, then you can keep your overhead low. However, I would recommend you at least put on a Sausage or Hotdog Sizzle and sell drinks.

To keep families around, you may also wish to provide a Jumping Castle or Face Painting depending upon your budget and overall goals.

FUNDRAISING IDEAS

70.

MUSICAL MOVIE NIGHT!

Musical movies are chosen for the evening, and parents drop off their children for a few hours to watch movies and have pizza. Some of the newer movies have SING ALONG options which would also be fun!

Look back at #24 for other ideas and suggestions but feel free to use your own imagination and you could also adapt this idea into a family event by combining other elements on this list.

Don't forget to check with council for licenses, permits, insurance, etc.

FUNDRAISING IDEAS

71.

COLLECTING COINS!

This is an easy fundraiser to have ongoing. Simply create tins with your school label or team label on them and send them home with the children.

Families will be asked to throw in their spare coins and return them to the school.

Ideas for families and coins:

1/ Pay a coin to watch television

2/ Pay a coin if you say a bad word

3/ Pay a coin to stay up late

4/ Pay a coin rather than eat a vegetable you don't like.

After the expiry date, you will need a few volunteers to count and maybe even roll the coins before you take them to the bank (depending on where you live and bank requirements.)

There are companies, which can provide appropriate tins, which cannot be opened except for after the end day by the school or team, but this would increase your overhead.

FUNDRAISING IDEAS

72.

ART EXHIBITION

An excellent fundraiser, especially if you are a school. Teachers would be requested to have all the children in their classes create artwork which would then be put up in Art Exhibition fashion around the school.

Parents would be invited to come along and purchase their child's artwork to raise funds for the school.

Other than supplies, there is little to no overhead.

If you wish, you can add other items like food, wine, and soft drinks.

It is not necessary to seek out sponsors or donations unless you wish to hand out prizes and ask people to vote on their favorite artwork.

If you are a team and you would like to do the same, you may need to rent a hall and get the parents involved with creating the art. If your team is looking for a new logo or name you could have a competition for best design, which would make it onto uniforms, caps, etc. In this case, sponsors and donors would be recommended. See above Trivia Night for a recap on how to ask for donations.

Don't forget to ask your local council about permits, insurance, and licenses.

FUNDRAISING IDEAS

73.

DANCE COMPETITION!

As a fundraiser for a school or team, you could ask teachers or coaches to get involved. Ask students to as a group or individually create a dance of their own or a video.

Choose a date and location for your live event where the dances will be performed live or the videos will be show. You will need an MC for the evening and a sound system including a microphone. If you don't have a stage, you could arrange an area like the gymnasium or auditorium in which people stand or are seated around the middle area where the dances would be performed.

It would be a clever idea to ask for donations or sponsors if you require costumes and are working together as a team. Otherwise, see if there are some parents who would be on uniform creating duties. To keep it simple, teams could be color-coded.

You may also wish to hand out prizes. Ask for donations from local and national businesses. See Trivia Night for ideas on how.

As always don't forget to check with council in case permits, licenses or insurance are required for your event.

FUNDRAISING IDEAS

74.

PIE (OR OTHER CHOSEN ITEM) EATING COMPETITION

This doesn't have to be Pie - if you are concerned about promoting obesity at your school or on your team, you can be creative and offer a healthy eating option or you can use a competition like this to get your students talking about the issues they face in a fast-food world.

It could be celery or carrot eating competition but I'm not certain how many volunteers you would get. Carrot cake might be a good compromise.

Traditionally, you would need someone to bake a lot of pies. You'd need people to pay for entry into the pie-eating contest. You'd need bibs and napkins and cutlery (unless pie eaters wish to use their hands.) You'd need an MC for the event.

You could sell tickets; also add in other things like jumping castles, face painting, etc. Up to you what you would like to add from the list and/or how healthy or unhealthy you would like this event to be.

Ask for donations or sponsors if you'd like.

Don't forget to check with council to see if you meet all their requirements for your event.

If you're worried about promoting the health risks of eating too much pie, you could make savoury pies such as Quiche (Veggie optional.)

"We were going to have a pie eating competition but as a healthier option..."

Alternatively, competitors could choose which pies they'd like to eat, savoury or sweet.

It's up to you, but the most important thing is to know your audience to find out in advance the best fit.

FUNDRAISING IDEAS

75.

FANCY DRESS THEMED PARTY

C hoose a theme for your party.
Some suggestions:
BLACK AND WHITE
TOP AND TAILS
20TH CENTURY
EDWARDIAN.
Promote your event via the usual avenues including social media, newspapers, radio stations, events columns, etc.

Check with council before you do any of the above to ensure you meet all their requirements.

Once you have your date and location all sorted out, you can start to plan the event night and ask for sponsors and donations for items you can use as prizes. It would be worthwhile to add The Silent Auction item #11 and other items as you wish from this list.

You will need lots of volunteers to be on the look-out for prize-winning costumes. Then narrow it down to the top 10 costumes. Those people will be asked to go up on stage (or in front of the group) and people will vote on who should win.

Include drinks and food to make your event more social. Add elements from Trivia Night Item #1 to ensure a fun evening.

Don't forget to check with council in case permits or licenses are required.

FUNDRAISING IDEAS

76.

SUPERHEROES PARTY!

This is mostly for the kids, but adults also love to dress up - so you can make it into a fundraising event for all.

Incorporate a blend of ideas from #76 and ask people to attend your event dressed as Superheroes.

A twist might be to have the children create their own SUPERHERO using a unique skill which they possess.

Follow, pick and choose elements from #76 to ensure you have a fun evening and are able to include the elements you wish to include.

Don't forget to check with council in case permits or licenses are required.

FUNDRAISING IDEAS

77.

HORSE RACING EVENT

If you have a Horse Racing venue nearby, you might be able to organize your event directly with them. They will probably have a Party Room (or something like it) and if you have the budget you can have a catered event. You can ask for an entry fee, including, food, beverages, and a day at the races. Betting will be extra - they will need to pay for that on top of an entry fee and betting of course isn't mandatory for this social function.

If the facility allows it, you can ask for outside sponsors and donors for an add-on event like a Silent Auction or Live Auction. Both would work really well and increase your overall profits.

The facility you are renting from will be able to tell you what licenses, fees and insurance will or may be required but I still recommend you check with local council just in case. Better safe than sorry.

If you don't agree with horse (or animal) racing, then you could still put on a social function but using a steeplechase game or a game with animation. To do this, you would have to think out of the box and use your imagination.

Alternatively, you could do a sack race (with humans of course) and make this a part of your event with add-ons such as costumes and teams.

FUNDRAISING IDEAS

78.

SPORT EVENT SATURDAY (OR EVENING EVENT)

If there is a big sporting event coming up and you have access to a large screen television or projector you could sell tickets to watch the game as a part of a fundraiser. What you would be offering is a shared event with friends and family with benefits such as food, beverages, and fun games. Add on any of the other ideas on the list to increase your fundraising revenue.

Ask for donations of prizes for between games play fun!

To save money on food you could ask everyone who has purchased an entry ticket to bring along a plate of food to share. For this idea, you would set up a table and people could just help themselves. Food would be included in the entry price.

If you can sell alcohol (beer and wine) - you will need a license - then it would be worthwhile asking for donations. Alternatively, it could be a BYO Bring Your Own beverages event. If it is in the evening, best to make it an adult only event.

Encourage attendees to wear the colours, jerseys, hats, etc., from their favourite teams. You could also sell tickets for a Guess The Winning Score Game.

Search online for game sheets which you can print out for free or be creative and make your own.

Don't forget to check with council – you know the drill.

FUNDRAISING IDEAS

79.

MEMORABILIA NIGHT

I f you have celebrity items available for auction or silent auction, you can plan an entire event around it. If you have an institution, band, novelist, sports organization, etc., then approaching them for memorabilia to raise funds for your school or team might be in line with their community giving policies. Things that might work in your community:

- Signed Books

- Sports Jerseys/Jackets (Signed or not Signed)

- Celebrity Items of Clothing (Signed or not Signed)

- Sports Equipment (Signed or not Signed)

- Holiday Tickets/Train/Plane/Bus

- Signed Art by Local Artist

- Event Tickets/Seats.

Think outside of the box and you might get an unexpected win.

NOTE: Check with the parents at your school. Are any related to or friends with a celebrity or sports figure who might be willing to donate to your son or daughter's school or team fundraising event? An ask from a friend/relative is always a BONUS and 9/10 yields the best results.

You'll never know until you give it a go!

PROVENANCE!

The provenance for your item will be particularly important to the price you will receive for it. Make sure you have the letter from the organization (a copy) available at your event for display. Also make sure you know the value of the donation.

FUNDRAISING IDEAS

80.

INTERNATIONAL FOOD FESTIVAL

Multiculturalism enriches our community communities and we're all keen to try new foods! An International Food Festival is an excellent way to learn about different foods. To get to know each other better and to raise funds for your school or team at the same time.

This event is best held in your school or team grounds.

When you have everything in place, choose a day for your event. This can be an after school or all-day weekend event, depending upon what your goals are.

Ask parents to bring along a dish from their family's country of origin. If the children on your team or school aren't aware of the origins of their family tree - then this is a good way to start a discussion.

Ask everyone to bring their dishes at a specific time and have tables set up for all of the food. It is good if you can have tablecloths (plastic or paper are ok.) It is ok to use paper plates and plastic cutlery if you must, however using actual dainty cups, plates and silverware can add an element of a eloquence to your event. Decide what is best after considering what your budget is.

You can always request donations from parents of these items, but you must ensure that they will be easily identified so that they can be returned.

You can decide how you wish to raise funds:

- Cost Per Plate (decide of fixed menu cost per plate)

- Buffet All You Can Eat (decide on fixed menu price)

- All You Can Eat Including Beverage Table Service (decide of fixed menu price.)

- Sell drinks separately. You could sell tickets in advance for alcohol if you have an licence to sell it at your event. Buyers would present a ticket and receive their drink.

You may wish to incorporate other items from the list, but this should be an opportunity for community and for getting to know each other as a priority.

As always check to ensure you meet all community requirements for insurance, licenses, etc. Please refer to Permissions.

FUNDRAISING IDEAS

81.

DJ PARTY

Fundraisers with DJ's at the helm can be great fun for your guests and can also bring in a good amount of money for your school or team.

As always, check with local council to ensure no licenses, permits or insurance is required. Review the file called "Permissions."

When you are looking for a good DJ, make certain you check their references not just their website. The person who you choose, will either make or break your event because they will be both the MC and the music player, and they will be providing the sound system too. Make sure you check to see if the music they have in stock will work for your target customers. You may wish to create a theme for your event, ask guests to wear costumes with the theme.

Once you know the available dates of the DJ you want for your party, then start looking in the venue. Make sure you have enough room for sitting and for dancing.

Once this is all organized it's time to get donations and sponsors and to get down to the nitty gritty of your event.

There are plenty of other ideas you can use to raise money with a DJ Party. Choose the elements you would like to use. Review back to Chapter 1 and the chapter on Money to ensure you have systems in place for money handling, etc.

FUNDRAISING IDEAS

82.

ABBA NIGHT

You either love them, or hate them...but ABBA songs have definitely withstood the test of time. You could also include their movies, add sing-alongs.

Make certain your target audience is crazy for whichever band you choose, and it doesn't have to be ABBA. After all they will be listening to the same band all night for your fundraising event. You could hire a DJ or if you have massive ABBA (or another band) fans in the crowd and access to a sound system you could make this into a do-it-yourself event.

Don't forget to check with council in case permits or licenses are required.

FUNDRAISING IDEAS

83.

DECADE PARTY!

Choose a favourite decade and celebrate everything about it!

Each decade has different options to choose from!

Choose how in depth you want to go!

70s PARTY!

The Seventies were the time for Heavy Metal and Disco.

It would be best to find a DJ for your party, but if you have a parent who has everything you need in order to make a successful event and you have a sound system and access to it, then you could easily make this a do it yourself fundraiser.

Check out the fashion, hair styles, foods.

Don't forget to check with council in case permits or licenses are required.

FUNDRAISING IDEAS

84.

READ-A-THON

I'm a big fan of giving incentives for children to read more - and there are companies out there who can help you to make a fundraising campaign and they will do pretty much everything for you including sending along materials, but there may be a fee involved in many cases (or a percentage from what you raise) so please check out the details.

If you want to organize something yourself, then it is a doable do it yourself fundraiser. All you would need is to send home a sponsorship form similar to what you did for other events and to ask children to get sponsorship for the number of books they can read in a month.

This would be an excellent opportunity to get funding for new books for the school library.

The children will need to keep track of every book they read.

Payments can be made directly to the school by either cheque or cash.

Don't forget to check with council in case permits or licenses are required.

FUNDRAISING IDEAS

85.

PETTING ZOO

There are many companies who will assist you in organizing a Petting Zoo. They will bring the animals to you and assist you with all of the details. You need a budget for this, but you can sell tickets and get donations and sponsors for add-on events. Plan ahead as they book out fast! Alternatively, check what's happening at your local Zoo! They may have Events on the Premises to assist you with your fundraising goals and needs.

Don't forget to check with council in case permits or licenses are required.

FUNDRAISING IDEAS

86.

TUG OF WAR!

Ask people from your school to form teams. Ask teams to pay an entry fee. You need a large rope with flags on it and a pit dividing the teams. Check out your local hardware store.

Seek out sponsors and prizes for the winners and for add-on events.

Don't forget to check with council in case permits or licenses are required.

FUNDRAISING IDEAS

87.

MULTICULTURAL DAY

This idea incorporates more than just food!
Traditional costumes could be worn.
Dances, bands, live music – could all be incorporated from your community.

A celebration and lots of fun!

An entry fee could be charged to enter the event.

Don't forget to check with council in case permits or licenses are required.

FUNDRAISING IDEAS

88.

TWISTER PARTY (OR OTHER GAME OF CHOICE)

This game can be an excellent add-on to many other events.

In your school or team's newsletter or website, ask for a show of hands from parents if they would like to lend their copy of the game Twister to the school.

Each game donated should be labelled with the family name of the donor, to ensure they get their game back.

If you need more check charity shops. You could even include more board games to your event! And some live game activities too!

Depending on the size of your venue, you can then map out how many game sheets can be accommodated.

When the games are handed over to you, ensure the name of the family is recorded and the mat, etc., can be returned to the family in the same condition as it was provided.

Everyone plays at the same time in some rounds, in others there can be team vs. team participation.

In-between rounds you could set up raffles, and even a Silent Auction.

With each round of Twister, the last person standing wins a prize.

Allocate points throughout the event, so the person who wins the most rounds is the Last Person of the Twister Party and award an appropriate prize.

Thank families for donating their Twister games and return them at the end of the evening (if families are in attendance) or the following day at school, or at your next team training.

FUNDRAISING IDEAS

89.

COOKING PARTY

T eaching children to cook with supervision is always a good idea.

This could be a combination event with a Bake Sale or International Food Festival if your school or team is able to access cooking facilities large enough for a group to get together and prepare a wide variety of items.

Alternatively, this could be a do-it-yourself fundraiser, where the families invite other families from the school into their homes for a dinner party. Beforehand, they get together and cook up a feast and then later everyone shares in the meal.

Ask around to see if anyone knows a Professional Chef who'd like to get involved to help your school or team raise funds. Who knows? One of the parents might even be a Chef!

You could put together a menu such as:
- Soup

- Salad

- Main Meal with glass of wine/beverage

- Dessert.

Charge a price per head. This price can go up quite a bit if you have a real Chef preparing the meal and they are donating their time.

If you don't feel comfortable, you could request donations for your school or team.

Don't forget to check with council in case permits or licenses are required.

FUNDRAISING IDEAS

90.

NON-EVENT EVENT

For this one, all you really need to get your going is your imagination.

Choose an event you would dream of having in order to raise funds for your school or team, the bigger the better and then work out what it would cost you (time and money-wise) to hold such an event. Itemize every single item with prices beside them.

Now work out what it would cost someone if they were to attend your event. Examples:

- Buying a new outfit

- Hiring a babysitter

- Taking a taxi home

- Tickets for event

- Get a haircut/your hair done

- Have a manicure/get nails done

- Raffle/Silent Auction items.

Now work out an estimate for each item above.

Now put the two lists together and make them into an invitation and send them out to large donors, inviting them to your "Non-Event Event."

If you are able to get email addresses and create your Non-Event Event in a virtual invitation, then that is another expense you are saving and can now add to the list of savings.

The key thing here is, you are saving them money by not inviting them to attend the actual event.

When you deduct one list from the other above, after showing them how much they have saved, ask them to make that money a donation to your school or team.

Include on your invitation a coupon, which they can cut out and fill in the details.

You can then send them a Thank You and a tax receipt if applicable.

Don't forget to check with council in case permits or licenses are required.

UPDATE: PANDEMIC PERFECTION

This event is perfect for the pandemic time we're currently living in. Keep in mind though, that many businesses are hurting and may not be able to assist you like they once were able to due to social distancing and other pandemic restrictions.

FUNDRAISING IDEAS

91.

EGG RACE

This event should be held outdoors in order to minimalize the mess.

A fun but messy add-on to other major events.

The overhead is low; all you need are teams of players, spoons and of course hard-boiled eggs.

Charge an entry fee for teams.

Ask for donations for prizes.

Don't forget to check with council in case permits or licenses are required.

FUNDRAISING IDEAS

92.

SECOND HAND/VINTAGE CLOTHING FAIR

Wearing vintage and second-hand clothing is really in. And you can find some real treasures if you shop around.

So, why not make this fad into a fundraiser?

Ask for donations from your community. Post flyers you'll be collecting unwanted, nearly new, recently cleaned clothing to raise funds for your school or team.

Include a request in the school or team's newsletter asking parents to donate. Ask all parents to ensure the clothing is in excellent condition and have been cleaned and if applicable pressed. I know this sounds like a crazy request, but it will save you from having to sort through unusable items.

I recommend using the school grounds for your fundraiser to keep your overhead low.

You will need storage and plenty of time to go through and price all the items individually.

Check high-end labels on-line to compare prices. Yes, everyone wants and expects a bargain — but they will expect to pay a little more since it's a fundraiser.

Create a welcoming environment, where customers can really have a proper look at the clothing, see the prices upfront and want to try them on.

CHANGE ROOMS

You will also need to make a few change rooms. You can ask people to use the school loos or create them using curtains and rails.

FUN RUMMAGING

For things like t shirts you can throw them into a box and people will be happy to rummage.

Same with handbags, shoes, ties and with jewelry too.

COAT HANGERS

Lots of coat hangers on site can also really help in the display of goods. Ask for donations.

FASHION RACKS

Ask local stores if you could borrow one of their fashion racks.

For additional monies, you could rent out stalls to individual or store sellers.

Add on other elements like food, drink. If you want to go very big you could even incorporate a fashion show. Refer back to #44 for ideas and suggestions.

Don't forget to check with council in case permits or licenses are required.

FUNDRAISING IDEAS

93.

MOVIE NIGHT WITH THE CLASSICS

Oldies, black and white films are true classics! Why not turn one or two movie into an event?

For this fundraising event, you could choose classic movies in specific theme such as: Cary Grant movies, Marilyn Monroe movies, etc., or you could choose a certain genre like Comedy, Horror, etc.

Another option might be to choose a movie, which was first, made in black and white and has been remade more recently. Invite your guests to come along and spend the evening watching both movies and talking about them afterwards.

You could even add in the element of a Quiz with prizes.

You could incorporate food, drinks, and other games, for which you would want to seek out donations and sponsorship in order to keep your overhead low.

Don't forget to check with council in case permits or licenses are required.

"You give but little when you give of your possessions.
It is when you give of yourself that you truly give."
Kahlil Gibran.

FUNDRAISING IDEAS

94.

CHEESE AND WINE OR FOOD TASTING/SHARING EVENT

Partnering with a local winery or brewery could make this a lucrative socializing event.

A second partnership with a local cheese expert or shop will also make this a smooth combination for a fundraiser.

If you are able to involve one or both of these partners, then they should be able to assist you in all aspects of your promotion.

Add in other suitable fundraising events from this list to increase your chance of maximizing your fundraising event.

If you're not into Wine & Cheese or a shared Food Tasting event, you could turn this night into Pizza & Beer.

Alternatively, you could create a Virgin Drinks (no alcohol) and Cheese Event.

For a kid friendly evening Pop (Soft Drinks) & Pizza might also work well.

Don't forget to check with council in case permits or licenses are required.

FUNDRAISING IDEAS

95.

PAMPERING EVENT

A sk parents if they have affiliations with small businesses who specialize in manicures, pedicures, and massages if they would help out in a fundraising event.

They would donate their time for a day in order to raise funds for your school or team.

Negotiate terms with them...Will they donate all or part of their profits?

If you theme your event such as a Mother and Daughter Day out, or Father and Son Day out it could work very well.

Consider adding appropriate services for your audience such as hair styling (trim, cut and blow dry, braiding, etc.)

Don't forget to check with council in case permits or licenses are required.

FUNDRAISING IDEAS

96.

MAKE OVER PARTY

F or this event, you might be lucky and have a parent at your school or on your team who is an expert in doing makeovers and would be willing to help-out with your fundraising event.

If not, you will have to work something out with a local spa or salon.

Once you get those details sorted, you could sell raffle tickets - the winner would win a full make-over.

You could ask for donations for other prizes, so there would be more than one winner.

Don't forget to check with council in case permits or licenses are required.

FUNDRAISING IDEAS

97.

TOMBOLA EVENT!

This is like a Mystery Prize event - where people make bids on items, which they cannot see - to raise funds for your school or team.

You go about getting donations as we have seen in the list above.

Bidders take a chance on what is inside of the box and decide how much they would like to bid. Some get really fantastic, donated prizes; some get small or even funny prizes.

The key thing is that everyone is a winner.

Don't forget to check with council in case permits or licenses are required.

FUNDRAISING IDEAS

98.

HOLIDAY RAFFLE

Raffles are excellent add-ons to any event, but they can also be extremely helpful and easy to organize for any holiday.

The advantage is that most people will be looking forward to and celebrating the exact same event, but don't let that stop you. If you want to hold a raffle and create your own holiday or event, go ahead.

Before you can hold your raffle, you have to get some donations of prizes. The bigger and the more prizes the better.

Best way is to make up tickets using a template you can find online and print them out.

Make sure you print the name and address of all ticket purchasers and keep the stub of the ticket in your book for records.

A draw should be held in an agreed upon public place and the winners should be notified immediately and prizes handed out or picked up.

Don't forget to check with council in case permits or licenses are required.

FUNDRAISING IDEAS

99.

RUBBER DUCK RACE!

For this one, you don't need a river nearby, but if you have one in your town then it'll be more to organise, but heaps of fun!

Using a river, you'd need to cordon off an area for the ducks to be dropped into the water after numbers are placed upon them...If this sounds too dangerous or too much to think about, please use the next option.

NEXT OPTION

You could have a few small children's plastic swimming pools, and it would work fine.

You would need to purchase some rubber ducks from the dollar store or a toy store. How many will depend upon how many prizes you are able to get donated.

Make a list of all the prizes.

Choose a duck and write a number on it.

The person who chooses the duck will win the prize, which matches the number. It's a race to find the winning number, not a race to cross the finish line.

Once you have the ducks with numbers on them, at the event you can float them, and people can choose their own duck.

Make sure you use a marker that won't come off in the water.

You can run this promotion regularly if it works well; so, don't worry that writing on the ducks will spoil them.

Don't forget to check with council in case permits or licenses are required.

FUNDRAISING IDEAS

100.

GAME NIGHT

We talked about this previously, but, the sky's the limit.

Just like #53 but only at nighttime and this time you can have an array of games or one particular theme depending what games are popular in the community.

Check the other fundraising ideas on the list for other nighttime events and add-ons to maximise your fundraising opportunities.

Don't forget to check with council in case permits or licenses are required.

FUNDRAISING IDEAS

101.

DOOR PRIZES AND RAFFLES!

An excellent way to raise extra funds when people are buying their tickets to your event is to have raffles set up for items that have come in as donations.

Alternatively, you can seek out specific items to be used as Door Prizes such as trips, vacations, hotel stays, cottage rentals, etc. These items are generally worth quite a lot of money; hence the temptation to buy a ticket with the prospect of winning at least one of these prizes would add to the excitement of the evening.

It's also an opportunity for you to ask your guests to print their names, addresses and phone numbers so that you can call them should they win (and not be in attendance.)

Or, if you prefer you may wish to hold our Raffle stating that the winner must be present at your event to win.

There are advantages to establishing a list of names and addresses, but if your event were in-house (at your school or with your team) then this information would most likely already be available to you.

Establish a list, which you could use for communicating (if the Principal or Coach agrees) with potential volunteers, other event attendees, etc.

Don't forget to check with council in case permits or licenses are required.

FUNDRAISING IDEAS

102.

LOCAL AND CORPORATE BUSINESSES INVOLVEMENT

Business Lunch/Dinner

Whether you are fundraising for a school or a team, the parents of the children will have connections to Local & Corporate Businesses.

This could be an opportunity for you to hold a fundraising event and allow these businesses to network and get to know each other in a professional forum.

If you are fundraising for a school, this could be an add-on event to a What Do You Want To Be When You Grow Up.

The businesses could pay a fee for lunch and then set up display booths. The children could find out what the different businesses do. You could ask for some of the businesses to speak about what they do and why it is important.

This has potential for a scholarship fund to be set up and/or major donations and sponsors through partnership.

Don't forget to check with council in case permits or licenses are required.

FUNDRAISING IDEAS

103.

PARTNER WITH ANOTHER CHARITY OR GROUP

True, you are raising funds for your child's school or team, but you are a part of a larger community and by working together you can help others to achieve their goals too.

This also widens the scope for your children, and as they grow you will be teaching them an invaluable lesson.

It's a win win situation - networking and combining resources.

Don't forget to check with council in case permits or licenses are required.

INSPIRATION

"Being good is commendable, but only when it is combined with doing good is it useful."
Stephen King

"Do your little bit of good where you are; it's those little bits of good put together that overwhelm the world."
Desmond Tutu

"If you want to lift yourself up, lift up someone else."
Booker T. Washington

ACKNOWLEDGMENTS

Dear Readers,

I would like to take this opportunity to thank each and every one of the parents who have helped me over the years on any/all events.

I couldn't have done it without you!

Thank you to my Mentors (you know who you are) for your encouragement, confidence, and faith in me.

I leave you with these wise words from Henry Ford:

"Coming together is a beginning. Keeping together is progress.

Working together is success."

I wish you success and hope this book helps you along the way.

All the best,

Cathy McGough

INSPIRATION

"Teamwork is the ability to work together.
toward a common vision. The ability to direct individual
accomplishment toward organizational objectives.
It is a fuel that allows common people to attain uncommon
results."
Andrew Carnegie
"The miracle is not that we do this work,
but that we are happy to do it."
Mother Teresa

ABOUT THE AUTHOR

Cathy McGough is a Canadian author whose work spans children's literature; young adult fiction; literary fiction; psychological thrillers; poetry; short stories and non-fiction. She lives and writes in Ontario, Canada with her family.

INSPIRATION

"Whatever we accomplish belongs to our
entire group, a tribute to our combined effort."
Walt Disney
"Those who can do, do.
Those who can do more, volunteer."
Author Unknown
"I can no other answer make,
but THANKS, and THANKS."
William Shakespeare

ALSO BY:

FICTION
RIBBY'S SECRET; EVERYONE'S CHILD
SHORT STORIES
13 (THIRTEEN) SHORT STORIES:
(Includes: The Umbrella and the Wind; Margaret's
Revelation;
Dandelion Wine (READERS' FAVOURITE BOOK AWARD
FINALIST))
LITERARY FICTION
Interviews With Legendary Writers From Beyond
(2ND PLACE BEST LITERARY REFERENCE 2016
METAMORPH PUBLISHING)
POETRY
PAINTING WITH WORDS – A POETRY COLLECTION
YA
E-Z DICKENS SUPERHERO SERIES (BOOKS ONE TO
FOUR)
A MATHEMATICAL STATE OF GRACE COMPLETE
SERIES (BOOKS ONE AND TWO)
+
CHILDREN'S BOOKS.

INSPIRATION

"The best way to find yourself...
is to lose yourself
in the service of others."
M. Gandhi

"Life's most persistent and urgent question is:
what are you doing for others?"
Martin Luther King